THE GLOBAL REFUGEE CRISIS

FLEEING CONFLICT AND VIOLENCE

STEPHANIE SAMMARTINO McPHERSON

TWENTY-FIRST CENTURY BOOKS / MINNEAPOLIS

Dedication: In memory of my grandfathers, Joseph Sammartino and Angelo Zanghi, who immigrated to the United States as young men and gave their loyalty, talents, and love to their new country

Acknowledgments: I would like to thank Jean Pierre Balikunkiko for generously sharing his story of courage and hope.

I would also like to thank Mayor Edward "Ted" Terry of Clarkston, Georgia; Harriet Kuhr, director of the Charlottesville and Richmond, Virginia, International Rescue Committee (IRC); Stephen Allen, site manager at the Richmond IRC; and Marie Marquardt, cochair of El Refugio, Lumpkin, Georgia, for sharing their knowledge and expertise. Thank you to Jennifer Snider, Director of Social Ministry at Saint Edward's Church, for helping with contacts. Special thanks to my fantastic editors, Domenica Di Piazza and Anna Kasik, for their invaluable guidance and insight and to my wonderful husband, Richard, for his constant support and encouragement.

Twenty-First Century Books
A division of Lerner Publishing Group, Inc.
241 First Avenue North
Minneapolis, MN 55401 USA

For reading levels and more information, look up this title at www.lernerbooks.com.

Main body text set in Adobe Garamond Pro 11/15.
Typeface provided by Adobe Systems.

Library of Congress Cataloging-in-Publication Data

Names: McPherson, Stephanie Sammartino, author.
Title: The global refugee crisis : fleeing conflict and violence / Stephanie Sammartino McPherson.
Description: Minneapolis : Twenty-First Century Books, [2019] | Includes bibliographical references and index. |
Identifiers: LCCN 2018016059 (print) | LCCN 2018022221 (ebook) |
    ISBN 9781541543942 (eb pdf) | ISBN 9781541528116 (lb : alk. paper)
Subjects: LCSH: Refugees—Juvenile literature. | Refugees—Social conditions—21st century—Juvenile literature. | Emigration and immigration—Government policy—Juvenile literature.
Classification: LCC HV640 (ebook) | LCC HV640 .M42185 2019 (print) | DDC 362.87—dc23

LC record available at https://lccn.loc.gov/2018016059

Manufactured in the United States of America
1-44687-35526-10/4/2018

CONTENTS

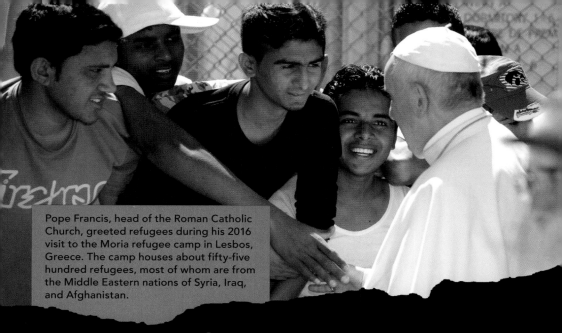

Pope Francis, head of the Roman Catholic Church, greeted refugees during his 2016 visit to the Moria refugee camp in Lesbos, Greece. The camp houses about fifty-five hundred refugees, most of whom are from the Middle Eastern nations of Syria, Iraq, and Afghanistan.

CHAPTER ONE

"WE WANT FREEDOM"

The Moria refugee camp on the Greek island of Lesbos had changed within days. The walls were freshly whitewashed. The sewer system had been replaced. And the camp's residents were moved so the camp, which housed thousands of people, would not appear overcrowded.

But nothing could mask the desperation of the people who lined up in the middle of the camp on April 16, 2016. Many people carried signs that read, "We Want Freedom," and "Please help." Some were crying. Several children had drawn pictures. In one picture, children were drowning in the ocean. In another, the sun was crying.

Three religious leaders, including Pope Francis, the leader of the Roman Catholic Church, had come to Lesbos to draw the world's attention to the refugee crisis. Since summer 2015, hundreds of thousands of refugees, fleeing war and persecution in Syria, Iraq, and Afghanistan, had journeyed to Turkey and then braved the Mediterranean Sea in small boats to get to Lesbos. Thousands died in the attempt. Those who reached shore could make an official request for asylum, or political protection that guaranteed they would not be deported (sent back) to their country of origin. But processing the applications takes time. While the refugees waited, they lived in run-down, congested camps. Many feared being sent back to their homelands.

The three religious leaders greeted the camp dwellers warmly. "I want to tell you that you are not alone," Pope Francis told the residents of Moria. "This is the message I want to leave you with today: do not lose hope!" When the pope left Lesbos, he brought three Muslim families to live in Italy. Compared to the millions of refugees in the Middle East and Africa, it was a small gesture. But the pope hoped his action would set an example for the world. As the crisis persisted, he continued to support refugees. In a 2018 address, Pope Francis called for people around the world to show compassion for refugees and immigrants and to "make the effort to assure refugees and migrants, to everyone, a peaceful future."

Who Is a Refugee?

The United Nations (UN) is an international organization founded at the end of World War II (1939–1945). Its mission is to help create the conditions that make peace possible and enduring. This includes protecting human rights and delivering humanitarian aid around the globe. The United Nations High Commissioner for Refugees (the UN Refugee Agency, UNHCR) is an arm of the UN specifically focused on helping refugees. It defines refugees as "people for whom the denial of asylum [protection] has deadly consequences." War, violence, and persecution in their home countries force people to flee their homes.

"WE DID NOT WANT TO PARTICIPATE IN THE KILLING OF OUR BROTHERS"

Like many Syrians, Nour Essa and her husband, Hasan Zaheda, became homeless because of the civil war in their country. Their house outside the capital city of Damascus was bombed, and Hasan felt pressure to join the Syrian army. "We did not want to participate in the killing of our brothers," Essa said. Their only choice was to flee Syria.

They crossed the border into Turkey to the north with their two-year-old son, Riad. From there, they took a small, cramped boat to Lesbos, where they registered and found shelter in a refugee camp. To their dismay, they learned that the Greek government had just agreed to send most refugees back to Turkey. The couple had spent almost all their money getting to Turkey and didn't know what to do.

Youth volunteers with Sant'Egidio head out in Turin, Italy, to distribute hot meals and blankets to homeless people in the city. The organization, which has about fifty thousand volunteers in seventy countries, also helps refugees.

One day, without warning, a woman from the Community of Sant'Egidio—a Catholic movement of laypersons (people who are not ordained) founded in Rome—approached them with a startling proposal. "Would you like to leave this place for Italy tomorrow?" Daniela Pompei asked them. "You would be on the same plane as the Pope. You have to decide right now." For them the offer was a miracle.

One year later, the family was living in Rome in an apartment provided by Sant'Egidio. Nour Essa was studying at a university and working at a pediatric (children's) hospital. Her husband, a landscape architect, found jobs in a warehouse. Riad attended nursery school, and his mother had new hope. "Now I dream about a normal childhood for my son," she said.

If and when they cross the border into another country, they may apply for asylum. If the country they have reached approves their application, they receive refugee status.

Immigration laws differ around the globe, and each nation has its own rules. Refugees are only one category of displaced persons. People leave their homes and become displaced for reasons other than the fear of violence and persecution. Economic migrants, for example, are fleeing poverty and are looking for jobs to provide better lives for their families. Political reasons do not prevent economic migrants from returning to their countries of origin, and they do not qualify for help from the UNHCR.

Internally displaced persons are fleeing violence. They leave their homes but do not cross international boundaries. They seek safety within the borders of their own country. Internally displaced people do not register with a country or organization, so experts have a hard time determining their numbers. The Internal Displacement Monitoring Centre is an independent organization that provides information and analysis to governments and humanitarian agencies. The organization estimates that 31.1 million people became internally displaced in 2016 alone. So every second of the day, one human being had to flee home.

Climate Migrants

Politics and culture play major roles in wars and oppression, which often force people from their homes. Many scientists and politicians know that environmental factors also contribute to unrest. They say that climate change worsens existing conflicts—especially in the Middle East and Africa.

Climate change results from burning enormous amounts of carbon-rich fossil fuels such as coal and oil to power factories and cars. As these fuels burn, they release huge quantities of carbon dioxide into the air. The carbon dioxide traps the sun's heat, which raises the temperature of Earth's atmosphere. Warmer global temperatures have caused glaciers to melt, sea levels to rise, and an increase in the intensity of storms, droughts, and floods. Such disasters have a severe and negative impact on water resources, food supplies, and the ability of people to make a living in their homelands. Without enough water, farmers have trouble raising crops. Grasslands wither and die, and herders are no longer able to graze their animals. With fewer food sources, people go hungry. For example, experts believe that drought in Syria between 2006 and 2011 caused poverty and hardships that helped provoke the civil war there. Rob van Riet works with the World Future Council, which promotes policies for a safer, healthier world. He says, "Existing threats—like resource shortages, poverty, famine, terrorism or extreme ideology—are only amplified by climate change."

Even when climate change doesn't lead to actual warfare, related natural disasters have forced millions of people from their homes. According to the UN, climate or weather disasters such as drought or flooding displaced 22.5 million climate migrants worldwide between 2007 and 2017. In low-lying areas, such as in the southwestern part of the Pacific Ocean, rising sea levels endanger the lives of island residents. Some people have had to leave their flooded homelands permanently.

Although climate change affects the entire world, some countries suffer more than other countries. Prosperous nations such as China and the United States have high rates of energy consumption. They burn the most fossil fuels, accelerating the rate of climate change. Poorer nations in Africa, Asia, and the Americas contribute little to climate change, yet they are far more likely to suffer its most devastating effects. For example, tropical countries are more likely to experience extreme swings between high and low temperatures. Such swings damage crops and lead to food shortages and hunger. And higher temperatures cause the energy levels in hurricanes and other weather systems to rise. This can lead to high-intensity floods and devastating cyclones and wildfires. Poor areas of the world have few resources to deal with such disasters, and it may take years to recover.

Hurricane Maria, for example, ravaged the US territory of Puerto Rico on September 20, 2017. Scientists believe that climate change may have increased the severity of the storm, the fifth strongest to ever hit part of the United States. Maria knocked out power, flooded hospitals, swept away bridges and roads, and caused more than forty thousand landslides. Even before the hurricane struck, many Puerto Ricans were living in poverty. One year later, the island was still recovering from the storm. Estimates vary but, according to a report from George Washington University, almost three thousand people lost their lives due to the storm.

Tiny Tangier Island, 90 miles (145 km) south of Washington, DC, faces a different scenario. Lying in the Chesapeake Bay, the island is home to crabbers who make a living by catching and selling crabs. Flooding and erosion, the result of rising tides and climate change, threaten to completely submerge Tangier Island and nearby islands within one hundred years. A seawall around the entire island (extending an existing wall) could save the residents, but it may prove too expensive. Susan Conner is director of the Norfolk Division of the Army Corps of Engineers. "There is not a lot of high-value property on Tangier," she explained in 2018. Building a wall "is not economically justified."

The cost of relocating victims of climate change is also steep. Between the 1950s and 2018, rising sea levels have claimed 98 percent of the Isle de Jean Charles in Louisiana. Although fewer than one hundred people live there, it has taken several years and $50 million to arrange for their move to a town 40 miles (64 km) inland.

Seeking Solutions for Climate Migrants

"Climate change is the greatest security threat of the twenty-first century," Major General Munir Muniruzzaman of Bangladesh said in 2016. "We're going to see refugee problems on an unimaginable scale, potentially above 30 million people."

"I'M THE SAME AS PEOPLE WHO ARE FLEEING WAR"

Ioane Teitiota fears he is fighting a losing battle. A resident of the small island country of Kiribati in the southwestern Pacific Ocean, Teitiota keeps a vigilant eye on the seawall protecting his home. During the highest tides, water surges more than 3 feet (1 m) above the wall. Climate change has caused violent storms in this part of the world, and Teitiota fears he will lose his home.

In 2007 Teitiota and his wife, hoping for a safer future, moved to New Zealand. Eventually he filed a petition for refugee status that went all the way to New Zealand's highest court. Teitiota argued that rising sea levels put his family in danger. Despite a great deal of sympathy for his plight, the government rejected Teitiota's application because he did not face political persecution in his homeland. He was deported in September 2017. Shortly afterward, his wife and three children followed him. "I'm the same as people who are fleeing war," he said two months later in Kiribati. "Those who are afraid of dying, it's the same with me."

With the election of Prime Minister Jacinda Ardern in 2017, New Zealand began to work harder to help victims of climate change. "Surrounding us are a number of nations, not least ourselves, who will be dramatically impacted by the effects of climate change," she announced. "I see it as a personal and national responsibility to do our part." Ardern plans to create a special visa for Pacific Islanders whose homelands are endangered by rising sea levels. She proposes to start with one hundred visas annually.

Ioane Teitiota hoped to be recognized as the world's first climate change refugee. He and his family fled their homeland in the island nation of Kiribati in the southwestern Pacific for New Zealand. There, they applied for asylum but were denied and eventually deported in 2017.

The Nansen Initiative Protective Agenda, approved by 110 governments in 2015, identified ways to help people displaced by severe weather events and climate change. These include disaster preparedness, protecting migrants from violence and human trafficking, and ensuring access to services and adequate housing. In 2016 the Platform on Disaster Displacement was launched to implement the principles and policies set forth by the Nansen Initiative.

Climate migrants who cross international borders do not fall under the UN's definition of refugees. But the UNHCR supports both the Nansen Initiative and the Platform on Disaster Displacement and helps countries develop plans to protect people. Under certain conditions, it may even provide emergency relief assistance. Erica Bower is an associate climate change and disaster displacement officer for the UNHCR. She believes that the UNHCR and other humanitarian organizations must do more than manage crises as they occur. They must also promote policies to anticipate future disasters and lessen their impact. "It's overwhelming how much trauma already exists on this planet," she said in 2017. A Global Compact for Safe, Orderly and Regular Migration, finalized by UN Member States in July 2018, aims to help and protect all migrants, whatever their legal status.

Skyrocketing Numbers

By the end of 2015, the number of displaced persons around the world had skyrocketed to more than 65 million, the most ever recorded. That year, according to the UNHCR, an average of 24 people were fleeing their homes every minute. By 2018 the number had risen again, to 68.5 million displaced people worldwide.

The UNHCR estimates that one person is displaced every two seconds because of conflict or persecution somewhere on the globe. The world faces a seemingly insurmountable humanitarian crisis. But refugees are determined to find solutions. In the worst of situations, they refuse to abandon hope.

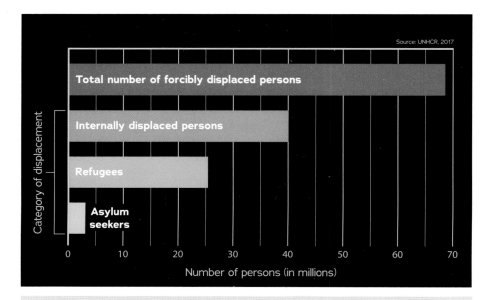

Total number of forcibly displaced persons

Internally displaced persons

Refugees

Asylum seekers

Category of displacement

Number of persons (in millions)

The term *displaced persons* refers to several categories of migrants. Of a total of almost seventy million migrants, more than half are fleeing crises within their own country or region. Another twenty-five million are refugees, or people who have fled their country and been given protection in another. A much smaller number (fewer than 5 million) are asylum seekers, or refugees who have fled but are still awaiting official recognition in another country.

Yusra Mardini:
"If Only Given a Chance"

Yusra Mardini was in seventh grade when civil war broke out in Syria in 2011. The next year, her family survived a massacre that destroyed their home. Yusra was a competitive swimmer, and a bomb struck the center where she practiced. Two of her friends died in the attack.

Yusra desperately wanted to resume a normal life. That meant leaving Syria. In August 2015, her parents arranged for seventeen-year-old Yusra and her older sister Sarah to fly to Turkey. There, they joined a group of refugees headed for Greece. Four days later, Yusra, Sarah, and a group of twenty refugees set sail in a flimsy dinghy. Within twenty minutes, the boat's engine died, and the tiny craft began to fill with water.

Yusra and Sarah jumped overboard along with two young men. No one else in the boat knew how to swim. The men eventually quit swimming in exhaustion. The two sisters battled the rough waves and guided the boat toward shore. They swam for three and a half hours. During that time, Yusra noticed a little boy watching her over the side of the boat. He was clearly terrified. Yusra made silly faces to distract him from his fears.

Finally, Yusra and Sarah brought the dinghy to the beach at Lesbos. Continuing their journey on foot, the refugees walked for days, sleeping in churches or open fields. After crossing to the Greek mainland by ferry, they passed through Greece, Macedonia, and Serbia by any means available—car, bus, train, or on foot. They arrived in

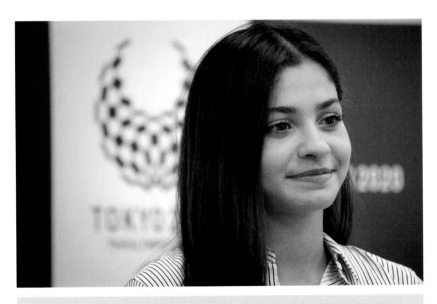

Yusra Mardini is a Syrian refugee and swimmer who lives in Berlin, Germany. In 2016 she competed in the world's first Refugee Olympic Team, where she won a 100-meter butterfly heat. In 2017 she was appointed the youngest ever goodwill ambassador for UNHCR. Her memoir, *Butterfly: From Refugee to Olympian—My Story of Rescue, Hope, and Triumph*, was published in 2018.

"We Want Freedom"

Budapest, Hungary—a journey of 1,573 miles (2,531 km)—while thousands of Syrian refugees were overwhelming the country. To halt their passage to Germany, Austria, or the Netherlands, the Hungarian government closed the central train station to refugees. Unable to use their train tickets, the Mardini sisters walked and occasionally hitched rides until they came to Germany, where they lived in a refugee camp for six months.

Soon after their arrival, Yusra made a special request. "We're swimmers," she said. "Can you help us find a place to swim?" The camp arranged for Yusra to work out vigorously with a coach. Her hard work paid off. In 2016 she was one of ten athletes chosen for the first-ever Refugee Olympic Team to compete in Rio de Janeiro, Brazil. She went on to win the women's 100-meter butterfly heat in Rio, and her story caught the attention of the world.

Yusra's newfound celebrity gave her a platform to stand up for refugees. She met with Pope Francis, US president Barack Obama, and other world leaders. She spoke at the 2016 UN Summit for Refugees and Migrants and at the 2017 World Economic Forum, where she was the youngest participant. In April 2017, the UNHCR appointed her as a goodwill ambassador, one of twenty spokespersons who call attention to the plight of displaced persons and promote refugee rights. "I am . . . eager to continue spreading the message that refugees are just normal people living through traumatic and devastating circumstances," Mardini said. "[Refugees] are capable of extraordinary things if only given a chance."

Many Jews from eastern Europe, including Russia, fled pogroms (violent mob persecution) in the late nineteenth and early twentieth centuries. About 2 million Russian Jews fled to the United States as refugees between the years 1881 and 1914. This Jewish family and their friends are from Moldova (once part of Russia). They are at a funeral during the Kishinev pogrom in Moldova in 1905.

CHAPTER TWO

DISPLACED BY WORLD WARS

One of the earliest records of a people forced to flee oppression is the Exodus of the Jews from slavery in Egypt, as described in the Hebrew and Christian Bibles. Throughout history, many other groups of people abandoned their homes in pursuit of freedom and safety. In the seventeenth century, for example, Protestant Huguenots faced persecution in Catholic France and left for England, the Netherlands, and North America. In the late nineteenth and early twentieth centuries, Jews in Russia fled their homes to avoid pogroms (mass rioting and violence against Jewish people). Before the twentieth century, however, international organizations did not exist to help uprooted peoples. World War I (1914–1918) changed that.

The global war between Germany and its allies and France, Britain, the United States, and their allies was one of the deadliest conflicts in history. Experts estimate the total number of civilian (nonmilitary) and military casualties at 16.5 million killed and 20 million wounded. At least another 10 million people were displaced. When the war ended, an international body known as the League of Nations formed in January 1920. The league's goal was to discuss world issues and settle disputes without war. Forty-two countries were part of the League of Nations. President Woodrow Wilson pushed for the United States to join the league, but Congress didn't vote to ratify the agreement. Many US lawmakers were isolationists. They didn't believe Americans should get involved in the affairs of other countries, so the United States did not join the league.

Nansen Passport

World War I caused millions of refugees across Europe to flee their homes. About that time, the Russian Revolution of 1917 overthrew the nation's czarist government (rule by monarchs, or royalty). The revolution led to the rise in 1922 of the Soviet Union, a federation of Communist republics. More than one million Russians fled the revolution, heading for safety across Europe. To deal with the

Fridtjof Nansen (1861–1930) was a Norwegian scientist, athlete, and explorer. He was also a great humanitarian, committed to helping refugees and known for creating a passport to aid refugees in their journeys to safety. For that work, he was awarded the Nobel Peace Prize in 1922.

This Nansen Passport was issued to thirty-four-year-old Paul Kasteruij in Bulgaria in July 1928. The document was crucial for refugees, who usually had no other form of identification.

crisis, in 1920, the League of Nations appointed diplomat Fridtjof Nansen of Norway as the high commissioner for refugees.

Nansen's task was exceptionally challenging. Europe was still recovering from the war. European nations were more concerned with rebuilding their economies and providing for their own citizens than with welcoming refugees. Native-born residents worried that large numbers of foreigners would create unwelcome change to culture and compete for jobs. Refugees feared they would never find a place where they could live in safety and peace. Nansen heard many tragic stories of people who had nowhere to go. In one case, 250 Russian refugees who had made it as far as Bulgaria were deported. They sailed in a small boat back to Russia, which denied them reentry. In despair, many threw themselves overboard. "Never in my life have I been brought into touch with so formidable [great] an amount of suffering," Nansen told the league in November 1920.

Nansen came up with a simple and revolutionary plan to help refugees. In 1922 he called for a meeting of the League of Nations in Geneva, Switzerland. At the meeting, he convinced the member states to honor a document later known as the Nansen passport. The certificate was available for a small fee, and refugees with the certificate could cross international boundaries without danger of deportation. By 1923 thirty-nine countries were honoring the Nansen passport. Eventually that number rose to fifty-two. About 450,000 displaced persons would receive the document and use it to enter other countries.

Tragic Failure

In 1933, only fifteen years after the end of World War I, Adolf Hitler rose to power in Germany as head of the Nazi Party. His leadership, brutal policies, and desire for domination of Europe brought about another world war. Hitler led Germany as a dictator. He and the Nazi Party promoted the racial superiority of ethnically German people. Under Hitler anti-Semitism (hatred and persecution of Jews) swept the country. Jews were no longer allowed to own land or businesses. Nazi soldiers removed Jewish teachers, doctors, and lawyers from their positions and

A young Jewish man in Germany cleans up debris after Nazis smashed the glass windows of his family's bedding shop. During the night of Kristallnacht in November 1938, Nazis targeted Jewish establishments across the Nazi empire.

seized Jewish shops. Jewish students weren't allowed to attend classes. On November 9 and 10, 1938, Nazis demolished Jewish synagogues (houses of worship), homes, hospitals, and businesses throughout Germany and in parts of Austria and Czechoslovakia. The horrific event was called Kristallnacht (Night of Broken Glass) because of the piles of smashed glass that littered the ground. The next day, Nazis arrested thirty thousand Jewish men and took them to concentration camps. In these cruel and hopeless prisons, people were abused, put to hard labor, and eventually murdered.

Although they didn't know the full extent of what was happening, people around the world expressed shock and outrage at the treatment of Jews. In the United States, Senator Robert Wagner of New York and Representative Edith Rogers of Massachusetts wrote the Wagner-Rogers Bill in 1939 in response to Kristallnacht. It would have allowed twenty thousand Jewish children from Germany, aged fourteen and under, to come to the United States. Many politicians and celebrities as well as ordinary Americans supported the bill. Opponents argued that it was not the responsibility of the United States to take care of children from other nations. "American Children Have First Claim to America's Charity" proclaimed an advertisement against the bill. The bill never even came to a vote. Isolationism, fears about unemployment, and outright prejudice killed the bill.

In 1939 more than nine hundred Jews, frantic to escape Nazi persecution, set out from Hamburg, Germany, on the German ocean liner *St. Louis*. The ship sailed for Cuba, but most of those aboard had filed for US visas (official papers from the US government allowing entry into the country). They planned to stay in Cuba only until they received the visas. However, the Cuban government had decided not to allow most of the migrants to enter the country. So the *St. Louis* continued northward to the US mainland, 90 miles (145 km) away.

Anxious but hopeful, passengers cabled US president Franklin Delano Roosevelt from the ship, with personal appeals for asylum.

ALBERT EINSTEIN: REFUGEE

Albert Einstein's groundbreaking scientific achievements in physics made him world famous. But because he was Jewish, he faced persecution and danger in Hitler's Germany. The Nazis seized his bank account and his apartment in Berlin. Einstein and his wife left Germany and became refugees.

After spending the summer of 1933 in Belgium, they sailed to the United States where Einstein got a job at the Princeton Institute for Advanced Study. He was determined to help other Jews flee the growing danger in Europe. So he signed numerous affidavits (official documents confirming a promise) pledging his personal financial support to Jewish refugees who wanted to come to the United States. His signature helped many obtain permission to enter the country. Immigration officials eventually realized that Einstein couldn't possibly fulfill all the pledges, and he stopped signing the affidavits. However, he continued to respond to Jews who wrote to him, offering whatever help and advice he could.

Albert Einstein and his second wife, Elsa, were Jewish refugees from Nazi Germany. Einstein was a brilliant physicist. Among other things, he formulated the theory of relativity, which led to a wide range of radically new technologies, including the global positioning system (GPS). He is pictured here at his home in Princeton, New Jersey, in 1944.

Their pleas went unanswered. Close enough to see the lights of Miami, Florida, the refugees were denied entrance into the United States. The ship had to turn back for Europe, where Britain, the Netherlands, Belgium, and France accepted smaller groups of the refugee passengers. Of these people, 254 would eventually die in Nazi concentration camps.

The Largest Humanitarian Crisis Ever Seen

Germany invaded Czechoslovakia in March 1939, and by the next spring, most of Europe had fallen to the Nazis. During World War II, more than six million Jews and millions of others (homosexuals, Romas or gypsies, people with disabilities, Slavs, Poles, and Catholics) were killed in concentration camps. The survivors of the Holocaust who managed to return to their homes after the war usually found them destroyed or occupied by other people. The new residents were rarely willing to return the properties to their rightful owners. Hostility toward Jews continued after the war in Poland and Slovakia. More than one hundred thousand Jews fled eastern Europe for Germany and Austria, seeking relief from the violence and persecution.

The war toppled governments and changed the face of Europe. By 1948 Communist regimes, under the control of the Soviet Union, had taken over many eastern European countries. Hundreds of thousands of people from these countries fled their homes. Some of them did not wish to live under a Communist government. Others feared that Communists would imprison or execute them for their beliefs.

Germans who had left Germany for other nations faced resentment and anger there after the war. People around the world associated Germans with the atrocities of Hitler and the Nazi Party. Even Germans whose families had lived in another country for generations were viewed as the enemy. For example, hundreds of thousands of non-Jewish ethnic Germans in Poland and Czechoslovakia were forced into internment camps before being expelled to other countries.

CHIUNE SUGIHARA

Chiune Sugihara was the Japanese consul (a country's official representative or ambassador in a foreign nation) to the small eastern European country of Lithuania. In the early days of World War II, he faced a serious dilemma. Thousands of Jewish refugees were surrounding the consulate building in Kaunas. Many had fled Poland to escape Nazi aggression, but the Nazis were moving in on Lithuania. Desperate to escape, the refugees begged Sugihara for visas. Three times, Sugihara cabled the Japanese government for permission to issue the documents. Each time the government denied permission.

So Sugihara decided to issue visas anyway. Often staying up all night, he wrote more than two thousand visas between July 31 and August 28, 1940. Japan then closed the consulate and ordered Sugihara to leave the country for a new post. As his train left the station in Kaunas, he was still passing out visas through the window. On June 22, 1941, the Nazis invaded Lithuania. Historians estimate that between forty thousand and one hundred thousand Jewish people can trace their ancestry to a recipient of a visa signed by Sugihara or his wife.

Chiune Sugihara (1900–1986) is pictured here in about 1940, the year in which he wrote—without official permission—more than two thousand visas for Jewish refugees in Lithuania.

"I took it upon myself to save [the refugees]," Sugihara said many years later. "If I was to be punished for this, there was nothing I could do about it. It was my personal conviction to do it as a human being."

At the height of deportations in Czechoslovakia, about 14,400 people were deported each day. Other ethnic Germans also fled or had to leave Hungary, Romania, and Yugoslavia after the war. By 1950, 11.5 million Germans had voluntarily left or been expelled from their homes.

United Nations

The League of Nations had not been very successful after World War I. After the horrors of World War II, a new international organization for peace formed. President Franklin Roosevelt, British prime minister Winston Churchill, and Soviet premier Joseph Stalin led a conference in 1945 to set goals for the new organization. These included an end to war, equal rights for all people, and international cooperation in solving economic and humanitarian crises. Fifty-one nations signed the charter, becoming the founding members of the United Nations. One of the UN's first tasks was to find ways to protect and settle the nearly sixty million people displaced by the war. In 1950 the UN created the UNHCR. The next year, the UN adopted the 1951 Refugee Convention, eventually signed by 145 countries. The convention defined refugees as those who have "a well-founded fear of being persecuted for reasons of race, religion, nationality, [or] membership of a particular social group or political opinion."

According to the convention, no one who qualifies as a refugee is to be sent back to a place where that person is endangered, a principle known as non-refoulement. However, individuals convicted of serious crimes or considered dangerous are excluded from this protection. The treaty lists other rights to which refugees become entitled based on how long they have been in a host country (the country that receives them as a refugee). These include the rights to work, housing, education, freedom of religion, and freedom of movement within the host country.

Originally limited to helping Europeans displaced by World War II, the UNHCR was supposed to operate for only three years—the estimated time to solve the refugee crisis. But other emergencies arose.

THE DECLARATION OF HUMAN RIGHTS

On December 7, 1941, the Japanese bombed the US naval base at Pearl Harbor, Hawaii. The next day, the United States declared war on Japan and formally entered World War II. Eleven months before the bombing, Roosevelt had called the nation's attention to the looming threat to world peace. By then Germany had conquered much of western Europe and Japan and had invaded China. Many Americans at that time wanted to stay clear of foreign affairs, especially wars. Roosevelt felt that this would be impossible. He outlined his goal for the world in a 1941 speech. He set forth four basic freedoms: freedom of speech and expression, freedom of worship, freedom from want, and freedom from fear. "Freedom means the supremacy of human rights everywhere," he said.

Eleanor Roosevelt chaired the UN committee that wrote the Universal Declaration of Human Rights after World War II. She was chosen because of her humanitarianism and commitment to refugee issues. She holds up a copy of the document in 1949. The General Assembly of the United Nations had adopted the declaration on December 10, 1948.

After World War II, his wife, Eleanor Roosevelt, chaired a committee that used the Four Freedoms speech to draft the Universal Declaration of Human Rights. Representatives from all over the world contributed to this document. The UN officially adopted it in 1948. The declaration lists thirty basic human rights. One of them is that "everyone has the right to seek and to enjoy in other countries asylum from persecution." The 1951 Refugee Convention would develop this right more fully.

So the UN periodically extended UNHCR's mandate (authority to act) until 2003 and then made it permanent.

Although the United States had joined the UN, it did not sign the 1951 Refugee Convention. But the US Congress realized that the masses of displaced people could lead to further conflict within Europe. So Congress voted to accept 350,000 displaced Europeans into the United States. In 1953 Congress went on to pass the Refugee Relief Act, which allowed an additional 209,000 Europeans to enter the country. With the passage of the bill into law, the word *refugee* entered US legislation for the first time.

Switzerland worked with the Red Cross to take in Hungarian refugees fleeing the Hungarian Revolution. Pictured here in November 1956 is Princess Gina of Liechtenstein (*left*) with a Red Cross worker, ready to help arriving refugees. The princess founded a chapter of the Red Cross in Liechtenstein (a nation that borders Switzerland) and was known for her humanitarian work.

CHAPTER THREE

"THOSE WHO SEEK REFUGE HERE IN AMERICA"

The refugee crisis didn't end with World War II. The Hungarian Revolution of 1956 again tested the world's ability to deal with massive numbers of migrants. In October 1956, thousands of people in Hungary protested against the Soviet-backed Communist government. When the Hungarian premier Imre Nagy tried to weaken ties with the Soviet Union, the response was swift and brutal. On November 4, armored tanks and Soviet troops poured into the capital city of Budapest, Hungary, to crush the rebellion. In the fierce fighting, the Soviets killed about twenty-five hundred Hungarians. More than two hundred thousand people fled the country, most crossing the border into neighboring Austria.

Austria responded with compassion and generosity. Austrians set up camps along the border and stocked them with food and blankets. They kept fires going to greet and warm the migrants. People around the globe watched the Hungarian drama unfold. This was the first world crisis covered on television.

Austria's interior minister, Oskar Helmer, declared that all refugees would receive asylum according to the UN Refugee Convention. He also asked the UNHCR for financial aid and for other countries to accept as many of the refugees as they could. Two days later, on November 7, France responded. The French Red Cross arrived in Vienna with medical supplies and returned home with a plane full of refugees. The next day, more than 400 Hungarian refugees boarded a train to take them to safety in Switzerland. Soon Sweden, Belgium, and the Netherlands were also welcoming trainloads of Hungarian refugees. In all, thirty-seven countries accepted almost 180,000 Hungarians. "It was the first movement in which refugees were recognized en masse," said UN high commissioner António Guterres fifty years later. "We had 100,000 people resettled in the first 10 weeks—which I think is inconceivable today."

The United States Responds

US president Dwight Eisenhower and other top US government officials thought it was important to make room for Hungarian refugees and others fleeing communism. Since the end of World War II, the United States and the Soviet Union had been engaged in the Cold War (1945–1991), a period of intense economic and military rivalry. Americans considered communism to be the opposite of everything their own country stood for. People in Communist countries do not have freedom of speech or freedom of religion, and they do not have the right to own private property. Many leaders and average Americans feared and hated communism.

But Eisenhower faced a problem in opening the United States to Hungarian refugees. In the 1920s, Congress had passed a national origin quotas policy that limited the number of immigrants who could enter the United States each year from any one country. The United States had only 865 openings for Hungarians. The number of Hungarians who needed resettlement was far more than that number. To deal with the emergency, Eisenhower used a special parole power to admit nearly 40,000 people. These parolees were neither immigrants nor refugees. Then, in 1958, the US Congress gave Hungarians official refugee status. Since refugees are people who face danger or persecution in their homelands, the law sent a message to the world that the United States believed people were not safe or free in Communist countries.

"An Asylum for the Oppressed"

The United States responded similarly for Cuba two years later. In January 1959, after a revolution of five and a half years, Fidel Castro and his army overthrew the corrupt dictatorship of Fulgencio Batista. Castro established a Communist government in Cuba. Many Cubans feared they would lose their freedoms and suffer government harassment for their anti-Communist beliefs. Between 1959 and 1962, more than two hundred thousand Cubans fled to nearby Florida in small boats. US immigration quotas prohibited that many people to come into the United States from Cuba. So Eisenhower and subsequent presidents John F. Kennedy and Lyndon B. Johnson granted the Cuban migrants parole status.

In 1965 Johnson signed the Immigration and Nationality Act, which among other things did away with national origin quotas.

Speaking next to the Statue of Liberty in New York, the president had special words for Cubans. He assured them that "those who seek refuge here in America will find it. The dedication of America to our traditions as an asylum for the oppressed will be upheld." Johnson went on to criticize communism: "It stamps the mark of a failure on a regime," he stated, "when many of its citizens voluntarily choose to leave the land of their birth for a more hopeful home in America."

President Lyndon B. Johnson spoke at the Statue of Liberty on October 4, 1965, as part of the signing of the Immigration and Nationality Act. The legislation eliminated quotas limiting the number of refugees the United States would admit from any one country.

One year later, Congress passed the Cuban Adjustment Act. All Cubans who set foot on US soil would be refugees from communism and would not be deported. They would receive permanent residency after one year without having to go through the regular asylum process. They would eventually become eligible for US citizenship.

Vietnamese Boat People

In another attempt to thwart the spread of communism, the United States sent troops to South Vietnam in 1965. After World War II, the Vietnamese people had fought to free themselves from French rule. The nation then was divided into the Communist North and the non-Communist South. Starting in the mid-1950s, Communist-controlled North Vietnam had been attempting to unify North and South Vietnam as one country under Communist rule.

US efforts during the Vietnam War (1957–1975) to fight for the

Almost one million Vietnamese fled their homeland in boats after the South Vietnamese government fell to Communist rule in 1975. Most of the refugees migrated to the United States, which had supported South Vietnam during the war. Once in the United States, most of the refugees settled in California (39 percent) and Texas (13 percent). Others settled in Washington State, Florida, and the Midwest.

non-Communist government in the South were a failure. US troops were ill prepared to deal with jungle warfare, policies were poorly thought through, and opposition to the war among the American public was fierce. In 1973 the United States pulled all combat troops out of Vietnam. Two years later, Saigon, the capital of South Vietnam, fell to the Communists. In the confusion of the takeover, the US government evacuated large numbers of Vietnamese who had worked with the Americans. Officials feared the new Communist regime would imprison or execute people who had supported the United States. So the United States brought military personnel and many well-educated Vietnamese people to camps that had been quickly built in California, Florida, Pennsylvania, and Arkansas. "To ignore refugees in their hour of need would be to repudiate [deny] the values we cherish as a nation of immigrants," declared President Gerald Ford, "and I was not about to let Congress do that."

Over the next few years, thousands of Vietnamese left their homeland. Cambodians and Laotians also became refugees after Communist takeovers in their countries. They set out in small boats.

OVERNIGHT TENT CAMP

Colonel John Haggerty had less than a weekend's notice. It was April 1975. Saigon, the capital city of South Vietnam, was about to fall to the Communists. In two days, one thousand Vietnamese refugees would be arriving at Camp Pendleton, California. No facilities existed to accommodate such a large group. In record time, members of the US Marine Corps set about transforming the barren land of the Marine Corps base into a camp with hundreds of tents and thousands of cots.

When the refugees arrived, many were in shock. "I cried. Everybody cried," recalled Loc Nam Nguyen many years later. "We had no idea where we were. We had just lost our country.... We had no idea what was going to happen with the rest of our lives."

The marines did everything they could to prepare the refugees for their new lives in the United States. They arranged for English classes, job training, dance classes, parties, and prayer groups and weekly Mass for Catholics among the refugees. The marines played games with the children and brought in fish sauce and other Vietnamese foods.

A young Vietnamese girl walks in a pair of oversized Marine boots at a makeshift camp created for Vietnamese refugees at Camp Pendleton, California. She was one of about fifty thousand refugees who lived temporarily at the camp in 1975 after fleeing the collapse of the South Vietnamese government that spring.

During the summer, about 50,000 refugees, mostly from Vietnam, passed through Camp Pendleton. Many found jobs and settled in Southern California. Some opened businesses or restaurants. Others established medical and legal offices. Loc Nam Nguyen became director of Catholic Charities of Los Angeles's Immigration and Refugee Department, a position he held for almost forty years. Others, like Viet Thanh Nguyen, wrote about their experiences in novels such as *The Sympathizer.* As of 2017, 150,000 Vietnamese Americans live in Orange County, California, just south of Los Angeles.

Many of the refugees died from starvation or drowning. The so-called boat people risked pirate attacks, tropical typhoons, and encounters with sharks as they looked for refuge in Thailand, Indonesia, Malaysia, and other Southeast Asian countries. These neighboring countries, unable to support so many newcomers, began turning them away. By 1978 news coverage of the boat people's desperate situation sparked anger and distress across the globe.

In 1979 the United States admitted 111,000 refugees from Southeast Asia. The next year, Congress passed the Refugee Act of 1980. It set the average number of refugee admissions to the United States each year at 50,000. The president, however, could raise that number in an emergency. In 1980 more than 200,000 refugees, four times the normal number of refugees, entered the United States. During the next two decades, the number shifted as conflicts erupted in different parts of the globe.

In the Wake of Terrorist Attacks

On September 11, 2001, terrorists from the Middle East attacked the United States, crashing two airplanes into the twin towers of the World Trade Center in New York City. Less than two hours later, both towers collapsed in the worst disaster in the city's history. Near Washington, DC, another plane flew directly into the Pentagon, headquarters of the US Department of Defense. A fourth aircraft crashed in a Pennsylvania field when its passengers overpowered terrorist hijackers. Almost three thousand people died in the attacks.

Reeling from the horrific tragedy, US citizens responded with grief, anger, and fear. None of the nineteen 9/11 terrorists had entered the country as a refugee. But at that time, many refugees were coming to the United States from nations such as Afghanistan and Somalia. These countries were known to harbor and train members of the terrorist organization al-Qaeda, which was behind the 9/11 attacks. As a precaution, President George W. Bush halted refugee admissions for two months. This time would allow the Department of Justice and Department of State to review the refugee resettlement program.

Meanwhile, the status of twenty-three thousand refugees already approved for entry into the United States was put on hold. These refugees included more than seven hundred women from Pakistan who had proved they were at risk of sexual and psychological abuse in their homeland. Although they had already begun their journey on September 11, the United States sent them back to Pakistan until further notice. Refugee children awaiting treatment in the United States for serious medical conditions were told they must wait to enter the country.

After 9/11 the United States created new and more rigorous security measures to screen incoming refugees and immigrants. For example, the Department of Homeland Security became a new agency. Three separate departments within it are Customs and Border Protection, Immigration and Customs Enforcement, and US Citizenship and Immigration Services. As part of their mission to protect US borders and enforce immigration laws, they screen and interview travelers from other countries and exchange information with other governments. Law enforcement agencies also built new databases that allow them to perform more security screenings and share more information with other agencies.

Over the next year, the United States significantly dropped the number of refugee admissions. Advocates for refugees worried about the sharp decline and its effect on refugees across the world. Lavinia Limon, executive director of the US Committee for Refugees and Immigrants, said in August 2002, "As the US is seen to diminish its commitments to protect refugees, other countries can feel emboldened to do what maybe they wanted to do in the first place." She implied that other nations might accept fewer refugees as well. In the fifteen years after the September 11 attacks, the United States admitted only eight hundred thousand refugees—a significant decline from previous years.

Compassion, Fear, and Prejudice

In the United States, as well as many other countries, public reaction to refugees continues to range from compassion and generosity to fear and suspicion. Some feel a moral obligation to help refugees and welcome them. Others believe the government should put the needs and safety of its own country first. Certain groups, such as the militant Islamic organizations ISIS and al-Qaeda, seek to harm innocent people and spread terror. Some Americans believe that admitting refugees from countries where these organizations exist endangers public safety. They fear that terrorists might enter the United States under cover of refugee status and organize violence on American soil. Those who support refugees believe that Islamophobia (fear of and prejudice against Muslims) should not prevent a prosperous country from helping those in desperate need. They also point out that refugees are carefully vetted (screened). The likelihood that a terrorist could enter the country as a refugee is quite low.

However, terrorist attacks in Paris, France, in November 2015 alarmed Europeans and Americans. Terrorists killed 132 people and

Parisians placed flowers and lit candles to memorialize the victims of the terrorist bombing at the Bataclan concert hall in Paris in 2015. One of the bombers carried a Syrian passport. In the United States, many leaders reacted to the bombing out of fear, pushing for more limits to refugee immigration to the United States from Syria.

MAYORS IN SUPPORT OF REFUGEES

After the terrorist attacks in Paris in November 2015, thirty US governors called for an end to the resettlement of Syrian refugees in their states. But many mayors across the nation—even those whose governors wanted to ban refugees—took a different stand. The US Conference of Mayors (a politically nonbiased organization of cities with more than thirty thousand residents) issued a letter to Congress on November 20. They urged lawmakers to "take no action that will prevent Syrian refugees from entering the United States after they have completed the screening process. . . . Our nation has always been a beacon of hope for those seeking peace and protection from persecution. We urge you to take no action that will jeopardize this rich and proud heritage." Sixty-one mayors signed the letter.

injured hundreds at six locations in the city. One of the terrorists carried a Syrian passport. This increased fears that refugees from the Syrian Civil War might be terrorists. Thirty US governors called for ending the resettlement of Syrian refugees in their states. However, these governors lacked the authority to block refugees. On August 29, 2016, the United States welcomed its ten thousandth Syrian refugee since September 2015, fulfilling a pledge made by President Barack Obama.

Travel Ban and Protests

The debate about refugees became particularly urgent with the election of Donald Trump as president of the United States in 2016. Within a week of his inauguration in January 2017, he signed Executive Order 13769. The order barred refugees and other visitors and travelers from Syria, Somalia, Iran, Iraq, Sudan, Libya, and Yemen from entering the United States for 120 days. These are all predominantly Muslim nations. Trump said that the new order would close the door to countries believed to harbor terrorists and give the United States time to review its vetting for refugees from those nations.

Angry Americans immediately protested the order, gathering in airports across the nation to show their support of refugees. Large crowds assembled outside the White House to express their strong disapproval. The protesters and many scholars believe that the ban is prejudicial, in that it specifically targets Muslims. Experts also say the ban is unconstitutional on religious grounds.

With the ban, refugees who had completed the rigorous vetting and counted on arriving in the United States suddenly found themselves in limbo. Those who had already landed at US airports faced possible deportation. Almost immediately, legal challenges began, including those by the American Civil Liberties Union (ACLU), an organization that defends human rights. At its request, a federal judge in New York halted the deportation of people stranded in US airports on January 20, 2017, the day after the ban went into effect.

Less than two months later, on March 3, an order by federal judge James Robart in Seattle, Washington, temporarily suspended the US travel ban. But Robart's decision didn't touch on whether the ban was legal. Furious, Trump tweeted, "The opinion of this so-called judge, which essentially takes law-enforcement away from our country, is ridiculous and will be overturned." Omar Jadwat, director of the ACLU's Immigrants Rights Project, disagreed strongly. "This ruling is another stinging rejection of President Trump's unconstitutional Muslim ban. We will keep fighting to dismantle this un-American executive order."

After Robart's ruling, Trump revised the ban twice. The third ban, issued in September 2017, affects people from Syria, Libya, Somalia, Iran, Yemen, North Korea, and Venezuela for an indefinite time. Legal challenges followed soon after. Judges in Hawaii and Maryland blocked the ban, ruling that it discriminates based on nationality and religion. On December 4, 2017, however, the US Supreme Court ruled that the ban could go into effect while lawsuits made their way through federal appeals courts.

A woman holds a banner against Trump's ban affecting Muslims as part of a protest in Los Angeles in October 2017. The travel ban, issued that fall and upheld by the US Supreme Court in the spring of 2018, limits immigration to the United States from several countries with majority-Muslim populations.

In April 2018, the Supreme Court heard oral arguments about the travel ban in *Trump v. Hawaii*. Lawyers from both sides presented their case before the justices. Two months later, the Supreme Court reversed the decisions of the lower courts in a 5–4 ruling upholding the travel ban. "The proclamation is expressly premised on legitimate purposes," wrote Chief Justice John Roberts, "preventing entry of nationals who cannot be adequately vetted and inducing other nations to improve their practices. The text says nothing about religion." So, according to the chief justice, the travel ban is legitimate and constitutional. The first five countries listed in the new ban are predominantly Muslim.

IN FAVOR OF THE TRAVEL BAN

Ever since Trump first announced a travel ban in January 2017, Americans have been deeply divided by the policy. Many continue to oppose the ban. But surveys show that about 60 percent of US voters approve of the third version of the ban. Most of these supporters are sympathetic to refugees fleeing war and persecution. But they feel that national security must come first.

Amanda Patrick from Georgia, the mother of a five-year-old boy, explained her thoughts to CNN. "The biggest thing for me, especially with having a child now, is the safety factor." However, she doesn't "have issue with the people who have been properly vetted," and believes the first version of the travel ban [which turned back refugees already on their way to the United States] was too extreme.

Eric Johnson, also from Georgia, does not believe a travel ban prevents Americans from helping refugees. "Let's work with the Red Cross and other international organizations," he told CNN. "Help those people who feel they're suffering as a result of ISIS and in Syria and let's try to support them. Let's not do anything to jeopardize our security, because if we are not safe then we can't help them."

Associate Justice Sonia Sotomayor read aloud her dissent, signaling an extremely strong disagreement with the majority opinion. Speaking for the four dissenting judges in a sharply worded statement, she said, "The United States of America is a nation built upon the promise of religious liberty." She mentioned a number of instances in which Trump expressed negativity toward Muslims. Although lower courts had considered such statements in their rulings, the Supreme Court did not. Sotomayor also made a comparison between the travel ban and a ruling the Supreme Court made in 1944, *Korematsu v. United States*. The court's decision in that case allowed the US government to continue holding Japanese Americans in detention camps during World War II. In both cases, she said, the government used an unproven security threat "rooted in dangerous stereotypes" to discriminate against large groups of people.

MALALA YOUSAFZAI

Malala Yousafzai was born in 1997. In her homeland of Pakistan, she stood up for the rights of girls to get an education. The Taliban, an Islamic fundamentalist political movement, controls some areas of Pakistan. They tried to ban girls from attending school.

In retaliation against Malala's support of girls, a masked gunman shot her as she was riding the school bus home in October 2012. Rushed to the hospital in critical condition, Malala survived and later was taken to the United Kingdom for extensive treatment and rehabilitation. Released from the hospital months later, she rejoined her family who were by then living in England.

Malala continues to champion women's education and refugee rights. On her sixteenth birthday, in 2013, she spoke at the UN. That year she established the Malala Fund, an organization that seeks to give all girls the chance for an education. On her eighteenth birthday,

Malala Yousafzai has spoken out against the US travel ban limiting immigration from Muslim nations. As a Muslim woman, she has fought tirelessly for the rights of girls and women around the world to get an education. Yousafzai was the co-recipient of the 2014 Nobel Peace Prize along with Kailash Satyarthi, a children's rights activist from India. In this photo from 2016, Yousafzai is speaking at a high school in Denver with a large number of refugees from around the world.

in 2015, she opened a school in Lebanon for refugee girls from Syria. She spent her nineteenth birthday visiting girls in refugee camps in the African nations of Kenya and Rwanda.

Malala reacted to the 2017 travel ban in the United States with deep sadness. "I am heartbroken that today President Trump is closing the door on children, mothers and fathers fleeing violence and war. . . . In this time of uncertainty and unrest around the world, I ask President Trump not to turn his back on the world's most defenseless children and families."

Bana Alabed (*right*) became known to the world through her tweets, which described her fears while living in Syria during that nation's civil war. She and her family eventually escaped the war in 2016.

CHAPTER FOUR
TWENTY-FIRST-CENTURY REFUGEES

Seven-year-old Bana Alabed from Aleppo, Syria, captured the attention of the world in 2016. Using a Twitter account managed by her mother, Fatemah, Bana documented her crumbling world as the Syrian Civil War intensified in Aleppo and bombs fell on civilians.

"We have no home now. I got minor injury," Bana wrote on November 28, 2016. "I didn't sleep yesterday. I am hungry. I want to live. I don't want to die." One day later, below a photo of a severely damaged building, she wrote, "This is my reading place where I wanted to start reading Harry Potter, but it's bombed." On December 1, she posted, "I am sick now. I have no medicine, no home, no clean water. This will make me die even before a bomb kill me."

Simon & Schuster published *Dear World: A Syrian Girl's Story of War and Plea for Peace* in 2017. It is Bana's account of one of the biggest humanitarian crises in history. The book includes chapters written by Bana's mother, Fatemah (*facing page, left*).

More than 220,000 individuals, including Harry Potter author J. K. Rowling, followed Bana's posts with growing concern. As the situation further deteriorated in Aleppo, Bana's Twitter account suddenly disappeared. Her followers feared the worst. They wondered if her family had been killed or captured by the military. Then, on December 19, the Humanitarian Relief Foundation, a Turkish organization that provides food and supplies to war-torn areas and to the sites of natural disasters, ended the anxiety with a post on its Twitter account. "This morning @AlabedBana was . . . rescued from Aleppo with her family. We welcomed them warmly." The relief was worldwide.

Syria: Civil Strife

The early twenty-first century was a difficult time for many people in the Middle East. They lived with high rates of unemployment and rising prices for food and other necessities. Countries ruled by dictators manipulated the economy to their advantage and to that of small groups of elite businesspeople. In this tense atmosphere, it took a single tragedy to set a series of protests in motion throughout the Arab world.

In 2010 police officers approached twenty-six-year-old Mohamed Bouazizi, who was selling fruits and vegetables in a rural town in Tunisia in North Africa. He didn't have a permit to sell his produce, so the officers told him to pack up his cart and leave. The sole provider for his widowed mother and six siblings, Bouazizi refused to leave. He needed the money. In response, a female police officer allegedly slapped him. Bouazizi was angry, disgraced, and desperate. He went to a nearby

Mohamed Bouazizi's mother (*center*) and his sisters Leila (*right*) and Basma (*left*) hold posters of him. The script on the poster at left reads, "The spark of the revolution, martyr Mohamed Bouazizi." Bouazizi died in early 2011 from self-inflicted burns. His death launched a revolution known as the Arab Spring.

government building and set himself on fire. That day people began protesting against the government in Tunisia. Images shared on the internet spread across the country, leading to further demonstrations. The protests captured the economic frustrations in Tunisia and quickly swept through the Arab world. The turmoil and civil wars that followed became known as the Arab Spring.

The next March, the Arab Spring came to Syria when a group of boys in Deraa spray-painted anti-government graffiti on a school wall. Many nations view President Bashar al-Assad as a brutal dictator. He had the fifteen boys arrested and tortured. Thirteen-year-old Hamza al-Khateeb died from the savage treatment. All over the country, outraged and horrified citizens took to the streets, calling for an end to al-Assad's dictatorship. Hundreds of thousands of people joined the demonstrations. Al-Assad, who is also the commander in chief of the Syrian army, authorized military action against the protesters. The military killed hundreds of activists and massacred residents of entire towns.

In response to the murder of innocent civilians and children, a number of soldiers deserted the government's forces and formed the Free Syrian Army to topple al-Assad's regime. Civil war had begun. As the conflict escalated, more than eleven million Syrians fled their homes, including more than six million displaced in their own country. As of 2018, more than five million of them have sought refuge in Turkey, Lebanon, and Jordan. About one million have come to Europe as asylum seekers or refugees, and about twenty-one thousand have resettled in the United States. Another several thousand have managed to come to the United States as asylum seekers and have received refugee status.

Eritrea: Political Repression

Syria is not the only country from which refugees are fleeing. Political unrest and persecution in Eritrea, Myanmar (or Burma), and other countries around the world have left thousands of people homeless.

PALESTINIAN REFUGEES

After the Holocaust, the State of Israel was founded in 1948. Almost one million Palestinians left their homes. The next year, the United Nations Relief and Works Agency for Palestine Refugees in the Near East (UNRWA) was created to aid them.

UNRWA gave refugee status to the children, grandchildren, and great-grandchildren of Palestinian refugees, with no limit on the number of generations that will receive this protection. In the early twenty-first century, the number of Palestinian refugees has grown to five million. About one-third live in one of UNRWA's fifty-eight refugee camps in Jordan, Syria, Lebanon, the West Bank, and the Gaza Strip. The rest live in or near towns or cities in these areas. Many depend on UNRWA for cash and food as well as health care and schooling for their children.

Residents walk through UNRWA's Beddawi Palestinian refugee camp near Tripoli, Lebanon, in 2012. With dwindling funding, the UN refugee agency has difficulty meeting the needs of the residents of the UNRWA camps.

Countries that belong to the United Nations almost entirely finance the UNRWA. Dwindling funds, however, have led to a steady decline in programs. The situation worsened when the United States, the agency's largest donor, slashed its funding in 2018. According to UNRWA commissioner-general Pierre Krähenbühl, the agency faces "the most dramatic financial crisis" since its founding.

Israeli leaders, however, feel that UNRWA is prolonging rather than solving the Palestinian refugee crisis. Israeli prime minister Benjamin Netanyahu blames UNRWA for stirring up anti-Israeli sentiment in its schools and institutions. "It is time UNRWA be dismantled and merged with the United Nations High Commissioner for Refugees," he said in 2017.

Many Palestinians depend on UNRWA. Ahmad Abu Salem is the owner of a small shop in a Palestinian refugee camp. "UNRWA is all we have," he said. "We don't have any alternatives if they continue cutting services. Without UNRWA we have nothing."

Eritrea is a small country in northeastern Africa that gained independence from Ethiopia in 1991. Twenty-five years later, Gaim Kibreab, a professor of refugee studies at London South Bank University, called the country the world's "fastest emptying nation." Between 2006 and 2016, an estimated four hundred thousand people fled the country. Refugees from Eritrea say the country is repressive and human rights don't exist there. Freedom of speech and freedom of religion are nonexistent. The government restricts travel and controls television, newspapers, and other media outlets. A widespread network of spies reports anyone critical of the country or its leader to the government. People don't know whom to trust. "In Eritrea you're even afraid to talk to your family," Sofia, a refugee who had made it to Cairo, Egypt, said in 2015. "The person next to me [in a café] could be a spy, and they are looking at what you are doing. People disappear every day." Those arrested may be imprisoned, tortured, or executed without trial.

An Eritrean man enters his lodging in 2017 in the new arrivals section of Shagarab refugee camp in eastern Sudan. Tens of thousands of Eritrean refugees live there. They are fleeing oppression, deep poverty, and mandatory military service, which often lasts a decade or more.

Only one political party exists in Eritrea. A constitution created in 1997 guaranteed certain basic freedoms and the right to vote. But Eritrea's first dictator, Isaias Afwerki (who is still in power in 2018), had little interest in the constitution, and it was never put into effect. In Eritrea the government requires all men and women to serve in the military for eighteen months. However, without constitutional safeguards in place, this service often lasts a decade or longer. Receiving a barely livable salary of two dollars a day or less, those in the military are often forced to do hard labor and are denied time off to see their families. The UN has called the Eritrean military "an institution where slavery-like practices are routine."

Many in Eritrea see fleeing the country as their only hope for a decent life. According to the UN, every month, five thousand Eritreans attempt to cross the border to seek refuge in a neighboring country. They must evade guards who routinely shoot at those trying to escape. Even if the refugees make it into Ethiopia or the Sudan, their actions endanger family members left behind. They may be put into detention facilities against their will. The government reasons that others who want to leave will think twice before risking the safety of those they leave behind.

Ethnic Cleansing in Burma

Burma (or Myanmar) is a country in Southeast Asia. People from the Rohingya Muslim ethnic group are fleeing Burma by the thousands. A minority in the predominantly Buddhist country, the Rohingya are mostly in the coastal western state of Rakhine. The Rohingya say they have lived in the area for more than one hundred years. Some trace their ancestry back to the fifteenth century. However, the Myanmar government considers the Rohingya to be terrorist intruders. They claim the Rohingya illegally came from Bangladesh when Myanmar was still a British colony. (Burma gained independence from Britain in 1948.) The government denies citizenship to the Rohingya, so they

VENEZUELAN CRISIS

A poor economy has sparked a humanitarian crisis in Venezuela, a nation in northeastern South America. Basic food and medicines are in short supply. Without enough vaccines and surgical supplies, the health-care system is unable to give patients the care they require. Medical staff can't even give necessary vaccinations, so diphtheria and other serious diseases are on the rise.

President Nicolás Maduro has imprisoned political opponents. He has appointed his supporters to the nation's supreme court, knowing they would block any attempt to impeach him. A new lawmaking body is packed with his allies. He has removed international news stations from the air for broadcasting news critical of his regime. Demonstrations against his repressive regime often end in violence.

The combination of economic disaster, health crisis, and political oppression have caused Venezuelans to leave their country in large numbers. According to a senior Red Cross official, at least one million Venezuelans have crossed the border into neighboring Colombia since the crisis began in 2017. Many go on to seek refuge in other countries, including the United States. In 2017 Venezuelans became the largest group of asylum seekers to the United States. Shannon O'Neil, of the Council on Foreign Relations in New York, believes that "We are potentially facing the biggest refugee crisis in our hemisphere in modern history."

have no nationality. They do not have the right to vote, and they are severely limited in their educational and work opportunities as well as their access to health care. Anti-Muslim sentiment and hatred of the Rohingya is so severe that soldiers have burned homes, murdered civilians, and raped women in Rakhine. The United Nations has called the persecution of Rohingya a "textbook example of ethnic cleansing"—the mass murder or ejection of members of an unwanted religious or ethnic group in a country.

Rohingya activists struck back on August 17, 2017, with attacks on twenty police stations and an army base. Twelve security officers died. In retaliation, the military launched a rampage, firing on people with

In the Rohingya refugee camps of southern Bangladesh, flimsy bamboo shelters sprawl across steep hillsides and valleys. The landscape is vulnerable to flooding from heavy rains and storms. Almost one million refugees live in the camps.

machine guns and burning villages. Within a week, 18,500 Rohingya abandoned their homes to seek refuge in neighboring Bangladesh. The number rose to more than 500,000 two months later.

Bangladesh set up facilities to house the refugees. But the camps offered only meager accommodations. Mark Farmaner is the director of Burma Campaign UK, a nonprofit human rights organization. He says the miserable condition of the camps is a deliberate attempt to discourage refugees. In October 2017, soldiers in Bangladesh even fired on Rohingya to keep them from crossing the border. Although Myanmar considers the Rohingya to be Bengali, the government of Bangladesh does not. "We are a small country with a huge population," said Najnin Sarwar Kaberi of the Awami League, one of two major political parties in Bangladesh. If the Rohingya "settle here permanently, it will increase unemployment so we can't give them the same opportunities as our citizens."

The next month, Myanmar and Bangladesh signed an agreement they hoped would encourage Rohingya to return to Rakhine. But most people believe that it is too dangerous to return. Widespread prejudice against the minority Muslim group is too strong for the agreement to be a realistic solution.

Only a First Step

After they cross an international border, refugees face an uncertain future. Where will they go? How will they find work, and where can they send their children to school? How will they create new lives for themselves? Escaping from their home country is only the first step. Further hardships and challenges await them.

DURABLE SOLUTIONS

The goal of the UNHCR is to protect the rights and well-being of refugees. But achieving refugee status is not a long-term answer for people fleeing conflict and violence. What does the future hold for them beyond a refugee camp or a meager, uncertain existence in a city? The UNHCR lists three possible outcomes that they say are lasting solutions:

Integration into the host country. Refugees may integrate into their host country, receiving the right to permanent residence and perhaps becoming naturalized citizens. Such an option depends on conditions and regulations in the host country.

Repatriation. When the danger is over, refugees may voluntarily decide to return to their country of origin. But they are not to be forced to return.

Resettlement to a third country. After undergoing lengthy vetting, refugees may be accepted and resettled by a third country. This can be a permanent arrangement or restricted to a specific period.

As of 2015, 145 countries had signed the 1951 Refugee Convention. They agree to provide for refugees who cross over their borders. The United States did not sign the original convention. But it did endorse the 1967 Protocol, which allows the UNHCR to work around the world.

Since 1980 the United States has admitted three million refugees through its resettlement program. During that period, other countries took about one million. In 2017 the numbers shifted. The United States took in only thirty-three thousand refugees while other countries altogether admitted about sixty-nine thousand refugees.

In this photo from December 2015, refugees from Burundi attend a rally at the Nduta refugee camp in northwestern Tanzania. Jean Pierre Balikunkiko and his family lived at the camp for a time after they fled war in their home in the Democratic Republic of the Congo.

CHAPTER FIVE

CROWDED CAMPS AND DANGEROUS JOURNEYS

Jean Pierre Balikunkiko was only nine years old in 2002 when civil war forced his family to flee their home. They lived in the Democratic Republic of the Congo, a country in central Africa. "The rebel soldiers came into the houses," explained Jean Pierre. "They took everything. The best way not to get killed was to run to the forest and hide." For almost a week

Balikunkiko's family hid in the forest. They slept on the ground and had little to eat. The only real way to avoid danger was to leave the country. So Jean Pierre and his family boarded a small boat to cross Lake Tanganyika. It separates the country from Tanzania to the east. During the night, Jean Pierre's cousin fell from the overcrowded vessel into the water. In the dark, no one could see well enough to rescue him and he drowned.

In Tanzania the family moved into the Nduta refugee camp. The camp—the size of a small town—is in Tanzania's northwestern Kigoma region, close to the border with Burundi. The Balikunkikos had shelter, but life in the camp was harsh, overcrowded, dirty, and disease-ridden. "We didn't get a lot of things to eat," Jean Pierre recalled. At first, the family lived in a tent with the bare necessities provided by the United Nations International Children's Emergency Fund (UNICEF). Over time, Jean Pierre's father was able to get materials to build a small, basic house. Officials told the children that they must never leave the camp. They might get lost or accidentally injure themselves. If they couldn't get back, no one would know what had happened to them. Jean Pierre and his family spent six years in the camp. Finally, the United States approved their application for resettlement.

Zaatari Refugee Camp

Few asylum seekers are as fortunate as the Balikunkiko family. Less than 0.5 percent of the total number of refugees are ever resettled in a third country. According to the UN, 86 percent of refugees live in countries that are close to their homelands. Many spend years in severely overcrowded refugee camps. Jordan's Zaatari camp, run by the Jordanian government and UNHCR, is one of the largest in the world. The camp was built for a maximum of sixty thousand people. But in 2018, seventy-nine thousand people were crowded into Zaatari. Twenty-four thousand basic premade caravans, or trailers, serve as

A Syrian family washes clothes by hand at the Zaatari refugee camp in Jordan. The Jordanian government and UNHCR run the camp.

living quarters. The camp has twenty-seven community centers, two hospitals, eleven schools, and about three thousand shops and businesses in the marketplace. Residents may start businesses or create jobs for themselves within the camp, but not outside it.

With a small amount of money, some business know-how, and creativity, residents of Zaatari have found innovative and practical ways to make a living. They provide a number of services including pizza delivery, bicycle repair, and a platform for e-commerce. They have opened food markets, restaurants, carpentry and handicraft stores, a garden store, and a bridal shop.

Besides filling important community needs and making money for their owners, these businesses boost Jordan's economy. In some cases, refugees and Jordanians have become partners, sharing the work and the profits. Taxis deliver goods such as pastries or clothing beyond the camp. Experts estimate that businesses in the Zaatari camp generate $13 million each month.

Life outside the Camps

Refugee camps have a limited amount of space. Eighty percent of Syrian refugees live outside camps, most of them in urban areas. There they have more choices and can seek jobs. However, many can find only menial, low-paying positions. They may struggle to support their families and live in inadequate housing.

A Syrian man named Saddam fled to Turkey with his extended family after their homes were destroyed in 2015. In Turkey the family lived in a deserted store without electricity or plumbing. Saddam could only find seasonal work in farming or the building industry. During the winter, the family would have to depend on their twelve-year-old son, who earned two dollars a day working a twelve-hour day in a bakery.

Refugees with more financial resources may have an easier time creating a new life. This was true for Abu Ammar and his family when they abandoned their home in Aleppo. In Turkey they started over, opening a successful shop that made Syrian desserts and catered mostly to other Syrian refugees. The family feels at home in Gaziantep, Turkey, where almost one-tenth of Syrian refugees have settled.

Growing Intolerance

Turkey did a great deal to accommodate refugees at the beginning of the Syrian Civil War. But the Turkish welcome is waning. Public opinion has grown more intolerant. Many people in Turkey—including the president—want to send Syrians home. "We want our refugee brothers and sisters to return to their land, to their homes," President Recep Tayyip Erdoğan said in 2018. "We are not in a position to hide 3.5 million here forever."

Syrians who live in Turkey face an uncertain future. Abu Ammar and his family have applied to become Turkish citizens. Turkish officials helped them when they started their shop by smoothing the way for necessary permits. "Now," said Abu Ammar's twenty-nine-year-old son, Mahmoud, "we are afraid Turkey will kick us out."

UGANDA: POOR COUNTRY WITH A BIG HEART

A relatively poor country in Africa, Uganda has opened its doors to refugees. "Uganda has the most progressive refugee policies in Africa, if not the world," UNHCR chief Filippo Grandi said on a visit in 2018. The small, inland nation keeps open borders, allowing free access to those fleeing persecution. As of 2018, it had welcomed about 1.4 million refugees, mostly from other neighboring African countries, including Somalia, Eritrea, the Central African Republic, Sudan, and the Democratic Republic of the Congo, among others.

"Almost 500 people a day come to Uganda," Grandi said. "All are allowed to come and receive protection, to mix freely, to work, to access basic services." Within days of their arrival, the government gives each refugee family a small parcel of land to farm. Their children attend public schools. The presence of so many migrants puts great stress on the country's economy. But a study done in 2014 in the capital city of Kampala showed that 78 percent of the refugees were financially independent.

Smugglers

Even when Turkey did welcome refugees, many Syrians wanted more freedom and prosperity than they thought the host country could provide. This was also true of those fleeing from desperate situations in Eritrea, Somalia, Nigeria, and other nations. Large numbers of people felt their best option was to move toward the European Union, an association of twenty-eight nations that function as one political and economic unit. The European Union allows people to pass between its countries without passports.

Since most refugees do not have visas, many become easy prey to smugglers, people who illegally transport migrants from one country to another. The smugglers purchase small fishing boats from local fishers

Desperate refugees sometimes turn to smugglers, who pack them into small fishing boats. If the water is rough or if too many people are on board, the boat may capsize and sink. Boats don't always have life jackets or inflatable rescue dinghies. So passengers try to swim to shore. Many drown. This vessel on the Mediterranean Sea in 2017 was crowded with migrants from Libya in northeastern Africa.

and pay the coast guard to turn a blind eye as the boat sets sail. The smugglers then charge exorbitant sums to refugees for the transportation.

Refugees who pay for passage may spend months waiting to depart. They may stay in cramped rooms with little food. Often they go to shore expecting to leave only to be told the boat has no more room. After refugees manage to get on a boat, it may not reach its destination safely. The distance from Turkey across the Aegean Sea to Greece, for example, or from Libya in North Africa across the Mediterranean Sea to Italy is not far. But both journeys are dangerous in the small, overcrowded boats in which many refugees cross the water. The boats can easily overturn in the water, and many people have drowned.

Operation Mare Nostrum

In October 2013, more than 300 men, women, and children, most from Eritrea, drowned when their craft sank off the Italian island of Lampedusa in the Mediterranean Sea. Out of about 500 passengers, the coast guard could only save about 150. Italians were horrified by the tragedy. In response, the Italian government established a huge search and rescue organization called Mare Nostrum (Our Sea). Rescue workers took groups of migrants to Italy, where they received medical care, food, shelter, and legal assistance.

Despite its success, many Europeans criticized Mare Nostrum. They claimed the program encouraged more people to risk the hazardous journey across the Mediterranean, thinking rescue workers would save them if necessary. Britain's foreign office minister, Baroness Anelay of St Johns, said, "We do not support planned search-and-rescue operations in the Mediterranean . . . they create an unintended 'pull factor,' encouraging more migrants to attempt the dangerous crossing and thereby leading to more tragic and unnecessary deaths."

TRAVEL DOCUMENTS

Most refugees do not have visas or passports. When they reach a host country, they have no legal means to travel to other nations. The 1951 Refugee Convention and the 1954 Convention relating to the Status of Stateless Persons addressed this problem by giving refugees the right to a Convention Travel Document. Issued by host countries, this document takes the place of a passport. It allows refugees (and asylum seekers whose refugee status has not been determined yet) to enter many (but not all) foreign countries legally.

Caroline Dulin Brass is a senior legal officer with the UNHCR. She points out that "as many as 41% of the world's refugees are believed to have no access at all to travel documents." This puts them at a great disadvantage. Travel documents allow refugees to visit relatives in other countries and to seek medical care they cannot get in the host country. They also give refugees a chance to attend school in another country or to seek a job.

The Belgian navy and the Italian coast guard rescued these migrants off the coast of southern Italy. The joint effort helped rescue about forty-two hundred migrants sailing across the Mediterranean Sea in rickety boats. The rescuers also found seventeen corpses on the boats.

After only a year, during which Mare Nostrum saved 130,000 endangered migrants, the program was shut down. Operation Triton took its place. Frontex, the agency that watches over the boundaries of the European Union, runs Triton. But instead of rescuing people, Triton patrols nautical (sea) borders to stop smugglers. Even without rescue operations, migrants continued to venture across the sea in rickety boats or inflatable dinghies. Without Mare Nostrum, many more refugees died.

"Beyond Desperate"

Some refugees do make it across the sea from Syria and other Middle Eastern and African nations to a Greek or Italian island. But once there, they must wait until the government approves their asylum application before continuing their journey to the mainland. With so many applicants, it may take months for the application to be approved. While they wait, refugees are jammed into filthy camps with few supplies and too many people. Camp Moria, on the Greek island of Lesbos, was built for about twenty-three hundred refugees. But by 2017, it housed almost sixty-five hundred people. Doctors Without Borders, an international medical humanitarian organization, has called the situation "beyond desperate."

Once they reach southern Europe, many migrants aim to settle farther north in the prosperous countries of Germany and Sweden. However, according to the European Union's Dublin Regulation, a 1990 agreement, migrants must make their asylum application in the first European country they reach. If they enter a second country and seek asylum there, that country can send them back to the first country. In recent years, Italy and Greece have received huge numbers of refugees and the "first country" pressure on them is tremendous. Both nations have called for a more even distribution of migrants among European nations. Despite several plans to reform the Dublin Regulation, so far, it is still in effect.

Germany's Welcome

In 2015 one million migrants arrived in the Greek islands from Turkey. That year Chancellor Angela Merkel of Germany announced the suspension of the Dublin Regulation in Germany. So when asylum seekers arrived in Germany, they could stay in Germany, even if it wasn't the first country they had entered. Germany agreed to process the asylum claims of all people who crossed its borders. Refugees would have a fair chance to make their case for asylum, even if not all claims were approved.

Many Germans applauded Merkel's stance. But the new policy provoked outrage as well. Protesters called Merkel a traitor and predicted that foreigners with diverse customs, ideas, and religions would weaken German culture. They also feared the refugees would take jobs that could have gone to Germans.

Merkel stood her ground. "*Wir schaffen das* (We can do this)," she repeated. It became the rallying cry for those supporting refugees.

SEXUAL ASSAULT IN REFUGEE CAMPS

Women refugees are among the world's most vulnerable people. Fleeing persecution in their own countries, they often become victims of sexual assault and harassment in refugee camps. Researchers from the Refugee Rights Europe have uncovered many instances of rape and of women forced into sex work. Very young women and girls have been forced into marriage. Traffickers have kidnapped women and sold them as sex slaves.

In 2017, 622 women from camps on Greek islands reported to the UNHCR that they had experienced some form of sexual and gender-based violence. This included sexual harassment, attempted sexual assault, and inappropriate behavior. Fear and shame keep many survivors of sexual violence from seeking help.

Poor, almost nonexistent security in many refugee camps contributes to the high crime rate. Poorly lit streets aren't well patrolled. Individual

Kakuma refugee camp in Kenya put up educational posters as one response to the epidemic of sexual violence against women in the camp. In 2018 nearly 190,000 refugees were living there, many of them having fled violence and instability in Somalia. Police patrol the camp at night, but there are not enough officers for the job, and most women do not feel safe.

shelters may not have locks. Women don't feel completely safe. "I am afraid of the snakes and the rats, the wild pigs," one woman said. "I am afraid of some of the people." The UNHCR has called for gender separation in shelters and bathrooms, better lighting, increased police presence (including female police officers), and more medical, social, and psychological services.

Turkish refugees cross the border from Austria into southern Germany in 2015. Germans are sharply divided on immigration policy. Many Germans feel the nation cannot deal financially or socially with the high number of refugees that arrive every year. Others believe Germany has the resources to do so as well as the moral obligation to help.

Soon about ten thousand refugees were entering the country each day. Many Germans responded generously. Citizens cheered for the arrival of refugees at train stations as they held welcoming banners. People collected and distributed food, clothing, and children's toys for the newcomers. Others volunteered to teach German or help with childcare. Hundreds of people signed up to host refugee families, providing living accommodations and helping them adjust to their new surroundings. But the sharply divided country also saw attempts to burn down refugee shelters almost every day. Those who opposed Merkel's policy insulted and threw garbage at the bewildered asylum seekers.

On one day alone, 13,015 migrants entered Germany. The huge numbers caught Germany off guard. Despite Merkel's best intentions, the country couldn't absorb so many migrants so quickly. Merkel was forced to reconsider her open-door policy. On September 13, 2015, Germany enacted emergency controls along its border with Austria. True asylum seekers fleeing war and violence would be admitted. All other migrants would have to show a passport.

GERMANY'S CHANGING POLICY

In July 2018, refugee travel through Europe became even more difficult. By June 2018, 18,349 asylum seekers in Germany had previously entered the European Union elsewhere. Responding to public pressure, Germany announced a reversal of its previous policy. Asylum seekers could be refused entry at the border—even before officials determined where in the European Union they had first registered for asylum. Transition centers, or border camps, would be built along Germany's southern border with Austria.

Refugees would stay there until deportation back to the first country they had entered in the European Union.

Immigrants entering Germany had slowed to about ten thousand a month by then. But distrust of migrants increased. Merkel felt pressured into the new policy so she could hold onto her leadership of Germany. "The security of our country begins at our borders," she said when the change was announced.

Angela Merkel, Germany's chancellor, was pressured in 2018 into upholding the Dublin Regulation. This rule, which Merkel had previously put on hold, turns away asylum seekers unless they can prove that Germany is the first nation they have entered after fleeing their homeland.

In March 2016, Germany began enforcing the Dublin Regulation again. Asylum seekers could enter Germany while authorities determined where they had first entered the European Union. If they had registered in another country first, they would be deported to that country. Meanwhile, they would be allowed to stay in Germany.

Stranded

Pressured by European countries that wanted to limit refugees, the European Union reached an agreement with Turkey in 2016. The agreement discouraged refugees from risking their lives to cross the Aegean Sea. Under the deal, Greece could return to Turkey some refugees who had crossed the sea to reach the Greek islands illegally. In return, the European Union agreed to accept the same number of refugees, arriving legally and safely, from Turkey. The European Union also promised to give Turkey six billion euros (about $7 billion) to help deal with the vast numbers of refugees.

Another event discouraging to asylum seekers was the closing of the Balkan route, a popular overland route that many refugees used to travel from Greece to Germany. Several countries along the way, including Macedonia, Hungary, and Austria, closed their borders and began building fences to stop migrants from entering.

But refugees continued to flee desperate situations. According to Frontex, 382,000 migrants from Asia, Africa, and the Middle East entered Europe in 2016. Although fewer migrants risked the passage from Turkey to Greece, the number of people crossing the Mediterranean from North Africa to Italy increased. More than 5,000 drowned in the Mediterranean in 2016, the deadliest year on record.

The closed Balkan route stranded thousands of asylum seekers in their trek toward northern Europe. Many found themselves stuck at the heavily guarded border between Serbia and Croatia. As of late 2017, most of those waiting were boys between the ages of twelve and sixteen, many unaccompanied by adults. (Girls seldom travel unaccompanied.)

"YOU CAN'T DO NOTHING"

Eric and Philippa Kempson are an English couple living on the Greek island of Lesbos, 6 miles (10 km) from Turkey. They remember October 28, 2015, as the worst day for migrants crossing the sea. A rickety boat approaching the shore exploded. All the passengers jumped overboard, including very young children. Babies floundered in the water.

The Kempsons, who kept a close eye on the sea, swam out to help with their teenage daughter, Elleni. She returned with a baby in her arms. Later that day, the Kempsons heard that a second boat had sunk. Hurrying to the scene, they discovered that the boat's deck had collapsed. Many women and children were trapped underwater. Greek fishers, the coast guard, and people from organizations such as Sea Watch and Greenpeace tried to save the refugees. That day 242 out of 300 people were saved.

Eric Kempson and his wife, Phillippa, help refugees who reach the Greek island of Lesbos near their home on the coast in Eftalou. He holds a life jacket (*left*) and a fake life jacket (*right*), a cheap imitation that is often sold to refugees. A real jacket could cost as much as $150. A fake jacket might only cost $15 but would be useless in an emergency.

After the European Union's deal with Turkey went into effect, the Turkish Coast Guard began forcing refugee vessels back to shore. But many people still risk the journey, and the Kempsons still help. They gather and distribute clothing, blankets, and toiletries to those who reach Lesbos. "When you see two-week-old children, people with cut feet and people who haven't eaten for days—you can't do nothing," Eric said.

Refugees from Middle Eastern nations follow a route across Turkey and southeastern Europe toward the countries of western Europe. The main route is known as the Balkan route because it passes through the Balkan region, named for the Balkan mountain range in that part of southeastern Europe.

Camped out in the woods, they watched for their chance to make it across the border. When the way looked promising, they sprinted with all their might, hoping to outrun the border patrol.

The children referred to their attempts as the game. But they seldom won, and the consequences of failure were severe. Guards beat them and took away their shoes. But the children kept trying. A twelve-year-old boy named Saddam Emal, whose story was featured in *National Geographic* in 2017, refused to give up, even after eighteen attempts to cross the border. He was waiting to get another pair of shoes before trying again.

In 1958 the Chinese government exiled Chinese artist Ai Weiwei and his family. He stands with his artwork *Law of the Journey* in Sydney, Australia. He exhibited it as part of the Biennale of Sydney, a major contemporary art event, in 2018.

CHAPTER SIX

WELCOME TO THE UNITED STATES

Acclaimed Chinese artist and activist Ai Weiwei knows what it feels like to be helpless. In 1958, when he was only one year old, China exiled him and his family from their home in Beijing. Authorities considered the views of his father, the celebrated poet Ai Qing, out of line with the ideals of the newly founded People's Republic of China. The government sentenced him to hard labor in a work camp and made him publicly criticize his actions and beliefs. Weiwei and his parents lived in a primitive underground bunker. They added to their meager diet by eating sheeps' hooves discarded by the butcher. "Our family were beaten and insulted, seen as the most dangerous species threatening the [Chinese] revolution," Weiwei said. When the head of China's Communist Party, Mao Zedong, died in 1976, the family was finally allowed to return home. Weiwei was nineteen.

Because of his experiences, Weiwei feels a close bond to refugees. In 2017 he made a documentary film called *Human Flow*, to call the world's attention to the plight of refugees. For the film, he visited forty refugee camps in twenty-three countries.

"The refugee crisis is not about refugees," Weiwei told the *Guardian* newspaper in February 2018. "Rather [the crisis] is about us." He believes that fear and selfishness prevent wealthy Western nations from taking in more refugees. "There are many borders to dismantle, but the most important are the ones within our own hearts and minds," he declared. Weiwei has given copies of his documentary to lawmakers in the United Kingdom and the United States. He would like to see these nations take a stronger stand for refugees.

Ceiling on US Refugee Admissions

Geography isolates the United States from the huge numbers of asylum seekers in the Middle East and Europe. They have no easy, practical way to cross the Atlantic Ocean. So these migrants must apply for asylum and be accepted before they come to the United States.

Since 1980 the United States has resettled about three million refugees, more than any other nation. According to practice, the US president consults with Congress each year to decide how many refugees to accept. For several decades, the number of refugees allowed into the United States reflected the volume of displaced persons worldwide. When the number was high, the country accepted more refugees. When the number declined, fewer refugees were admitted. But in recent years, admissions have not kept pace with the masses of people fleeing persecution and violence in Syria, Iraq, and Africa.

In 2018 Trump lowered the quota from 97,000 in 2016 to 45,000, the lowest number for refugee admission in decades.

"The security and safety of the American people is our chief concern," a government official who asked to have his name withheld told news reporters from CNN News. Later, he called the refugee limit of forty-five thousand "consistent with our foreign policy goals and operational capacity in light of additional security vetting procedures that we are implementing, and the domestic asylum backlog that [Homeland Security] is currently facing." So Homeland Security is more thoroughly screening refugees. The agency believes this approach will help keep terrorists out of the country. Since so many cases were already in progress in 2017, the new forty-five thousand limit was as many as Homeland Security felt it could effectively handle.

Many Americans do not accept the argument for cutting the limit by more than 50 percent. "It didn't have to be this number," said Linda Hartke, chief executive officer of the Lutheran Immigration and Refugee Service. (This church organization supports refugees and migrants.) "And it certainly doesn't reflect American values or the expectations of communities and local churches and the people I talk to all over the country."

Betsy Fisher is the policy director for the International Refugee Assistance Project. This agency works to establish human rights for refugees and displaced persons. Fisher also expressed distress at Trump's reduction. "We are abandoning desperate people in life-or-death situations, including children with medical emergencies, US wartime allies, and survivors of torture," she said.

Critics of the lowered ceiling pointed out that US vetting is already the toughest in the world. Even before Trump's election, extra vetting was in place for individuals from countries considered at high risk for terrorism. Of the 784,000 refugees resettled in the United States between September 2001 and September 2015, authorities arrested only 3 for planning terrorist activities, and 2 did not intend any action in the United States. According to the Migration Policy Institute, the plans of the other suspect were "barely credible" Yet in September 2018, Secretary of State Mike Pompeo announced that the United States would lower the "refugee ceiling" for the coming year from 45,000 to 30,000. This is the lowest it has been since the 9/11 attacks.

The US Vetting Process

The US Committee for Refugees and Immigrants lists fourteen steps in the vetting of refugees entering the United States. It involves background checks, interviews, and medical screenings. These steps ensure a person qualifies as a refugee, is being honest about his or her identity, and is not dangerous. "Of all the ways to enter this country as an immigrant, doing so as a refugee is probably the most cumbersome and time-consuming," Jeh Johnson, former secretary of Homeland Security, said in 2017. These are the fourteen steps:

1. ***Registration and confirmation of refugee status.*** Migrants who cross any international border and wish to qualify for asylum must register with the UNHCR, either at a refugee camp or an urban office. Officials determine if they meet the UN criteria for refugee status. If so, they would have "a well-founded fear of persecution based on religion, race, nationality, political opinion, or membership in a particular social group." Applicants are fingerprinted. Syrians may be given an iris scan for identification. (Every person's iris, or colored part of the eye, has a pattern as unique as their fingerprints.)

2. ***Referral to the United States***. After the UN Refugee Agency determines that someone meets the criteria for refugee status, the organization must decide whether to refer the person for resettlement. Only the most vulnerable are eligible for resettlement in a third country. These include women and children at risk of abuse and exploitation, survivors of violence, and those with serious medical needs. Separated families are considered vulnerable, and

so the goal is to reunite them. Less than 1 percent of refugees worldwide are considered for resettlement in a third country. Only a small number of countries participate in the UN Refugee Agency resettlement program. Prior to the Trump administration, the United States accepted the most refugees.

3. **US Department of State interview**. An official from one of the nine Resettlement Support Centers that the United States operates throughout the world interviews refugees referred to the United States. The official gathers background and personal information for the US Department of State.

4. **First security check**. The State Department runs the names of all refugees referred to the United States through the FBI's terrorist watch list. This database highlights people whose suspicious behavior has caught the attention of officials, who have placed them on the security watch list. These behaviors include crime or dealings with a terrorist organization.

5. **Security Advisory Opinion**. Some refugees require an additional check called a Security Advisory Opinion. A number of intelligence and law enforcement agencies review people's visa applications for signs that they might be a security risk. If the review confirms that they are a threat, their resettlement applications will be denied.

6. **Security screening and interagency check**. The National Counterterrorism Center runs a check through several agencies of all applicants within a certain age range. This check is repeated throughout the application to identify any new information between the first security check and the refugee's entrance into the United States.

7. **Syria enhanced review**. Because their country is a source of terrorism, Syrians go through extra vetting. If a person's story seems suspicious, officials pass the case to the fraud detection unit of Homeland Security.

WATCH LIST CONTROVERSY

The FBI's terrorist watch list is controversial. Not only has it failed to prevent some terrorist attacks, but it has also listed innocent people. If a person travels to a foreign country that has terrorist organizations or has friends or family already under suspicion, that person may be placed on the list. Some have no idea that they are on the watch list. Rahinah Ibrahim, a Malaysian architect with a PhD from Stanford University in California, didn't know about her listing until she was arrested and handcuffed at the San Francisco International Airport in January 2005. She spent more than two hours at the police station before she was released and told that her name was off the no-fly list. (The no-fly list identifies people who aren't allowed to board passenger flights to, from, or within the United States.) Ibrahim proceeded on her trip to Malaysia. But ten weeks later, when she tried to return to the United States, a supervisor at the Malaysian airport in Kuala Lumpur told her that the United States revoked her visa. She could not return.

One year after her encounter at the San Francisco Airport, Ibrahim filed a lawsuit to have her name removed from the terrorist database. Eight years later, she won her case. A federal judge ruled that she was entitled to due process (fair treatment) under US law. The government had no right to place her on a terrorist list without telling her why. But Ibrahim wasn't in court to hear the decision. She still didn't have a visa.

8. **United States Citizenship and Immigration Services in-person interview.** An officer from this agency travels to meet the refugees and their families overseas. The officer fingerprints the applicant and family members and takes photos. After carefully studying the applicant's statements and case file, the officer evaluates the person's credibility. Does the applicant's story reflect the reality of his country's situation? The officer then determines whether the person and his family truly qualify as refugees and are eligible for admission into the United States.

9. **Approval.** The Citizenship and Immigration Services officer conditionally (temporarily) approves a refugee who has passed the various steps. The officer gives the application to the Department of State for processing. Full approval depends on the security checks and medical screenings.

10. **Fingerprinting.** The FBI, Homeland Security, and the Department of Defense screen the fingerprints taken by the officer in step 8.

11. **Medical screening.** Applicants go through a medical exam to make sure that they do not carry any contagious diseases and are not a public health threat.

12. **Assignment to a sponsor agency.** An agency such as the US Committee for Refugees and Immigrants will assign approved refugees to a partner agency. That organization provides information and helps refugees adjust to life in the United States.

13. **Cultural orientation.** Before they go to the United States, refugees take classes to prepare them for their journey and teach them about American society and customs.

14. **Travel to the United States.** Approved refugees fly to the United States, where a US Customs and Border Protection officer reviews their documentation and does more security checks. The officer verifies that the person who has arrived is the same person who passed the security checks and was cleared for admission into the United States. If the officer determines that the refugee could be a security threat, entrance into the United States will be denied.

The entire application takes from eighteen to twenty-four months. The period may be longer if extra vetting is required or if officials have difficulty traveling to remote areas to meet with applicants. For example, during the rainy season of some parts of the world, airline flights may be postponed or canceled. Interviews are delayed. Applicants know that if vetting takes too long, their security checks will begin to expire. Then they have to start vetting all over again.

Arrival in the United States

Refugees do not choose where they will live when they first come to the United States. Their refugee resettlement agency makes that decision. It considers job availability, housing prices, and the family's unique needs, as well as accessibility to special medical treatment, if needed. If refugees already have family in the United States, the agency tries to place them near relatives.

When refugees arrive in the United States, a representative from their resettlement agency is usually at the airport to meet them and help with immediate needs. First, the representative drives the family from the airport to an apartment stocked with food and other basic needs. The next day often includes a trip to the grocery store. Many refugees have never seen so much food in one place before. Helpers from the agency guide them through the aisles, explain unfamiliar foods, and help them through checkout.

Within a month, the resettlement agency will help refugees through some crucial tasks. These include applying for a social security number (a nine-digit number that identifies a person and is required for legal employment) and enrolling children in school. The agency will also help families set up doctors' appointments, learn about the US health-care system, and find English language classes. After refugees have lived in the United States for one year, they can apply for status as a permanent resident alien. This grants them the legal right to stay in the United States. Citizenship and Immigration Services provides an identification card known as a green card, which confirms their right to live and work in the United States. Sometimes the fee for a green card is almost $1,000. Because of their status, refugees are not required to pay this fee.

A CHATBOT NAMED MARHUB

Sometimes refugees are confused or nervous about meeting with UNHCR officials. Many don't speak English or don't have words in their language for some of the concepts in the English-speaking world. They may not know that they can request their own translator. They may not know that they have the right to read a transcript of their interview for accuracy. The uneasiness they feel may even prevent some people from registering or applying for asylum. To help with these concerns, some business students from the University of California at Berkeley's Haas School of Business developed a chatbot called MarHub. The name is a playful derivative of the Arabic word *marhaba*, which means "hello."

Most refugees have smartphones and can access MarHub through Facebook. The program will one day be available on WhatsAPP and through text. Available in English and Arabic, MarHub leads asylum seekers through the interview process . Asylum seekers can type in questions through Facebook Messenger. The answers they receive depend on their country of origin, current location, and need to know about the legal process. Eventually MarHub will use artificial intelligence to reply more fully to a broader range of questions.

Migrants use Wi-Fi at a hub for plugging in their smartphones. They are living at a temporary shelter in a hall at a fairgrounds in Berlin, Germany. MarHub is a software program available through Facebook that helps displaced persons understand the process of seeking asylum. The program is available so far in English and Arabic.

Somali immigrant Jamal Dar arrived in the United States in the 1990s from Kenya. Here, he looks in on a civics and language class for Somali refugees in an office at the African Youth and Community Organization. He started the program in East Portland, Oregon, in 2009 to help Somali youths. Since then he has expanded it to focus on the needs of families as well.

"A Beautiful Day"

Five years after arriving in the United States, refugees may apply for citizenship. They must be at least eighteen years old and be able to speak, read, and write English. They must also take a naturalization test that covers US history and government. Twenty-three-year-old Myakim Chuol and her family fled their home in the Republic of South Sudan. They came to the United States from a refugee camp in Kenya. Chuol prepared for the citizenship test by listening repeatedly to a study CD. "I told myself 'No more listening to music, this is what you will listen to,'" Chuol explained. "It worked."

In June 2017, an emotional Chuol took the oath of allegiance to the United States in Omaha, Nebraska, with thirty other refugees from around the world. "There are so many things that can cause you to be hopeless," she said. "But this [naturalization ceremony]—this is a beautiful day."

"WE WERE SUPER HAPPY"

Jean Pierre Balikunkiko (*below*) remembers vividly the day his father learned that their family would be resettled to the United States. Jean Pierre was fourteen years old. He had lived in Nduta refugee camp in Tanzania for six years. Almost immediately, the Balikunkikos were taken to live in a nearby site for intensive monthlong classes about daily life in the United States. "We were super happy," Jean Pierre said.

After completing the classes, the family began the first leg of their journey with a flight to Nairobi, Kenya—their first airplane trip ever. Their second flight would take them to the United States. When they first arrived in Richmond, Virginia, Jean Pierre was confused. His surroundings had nothing in common with the photos he had seen of large cities such as Chicago, Illinois. "I did not believe we had arrived in the United States yet," he said.

Jean Pierre was old enough for ninth grade. But the school district felt his English was not strong and placed him in sixth grade instead. He was not happy about the decision, but he soon began to master the language. Jean Pierre later became the first person in his family to graduate from high school. In 2013 he became an American citizen. By 2018 he was majoring in international studies and social justice at Virginia Commonwealth University. Jean Pierre hopes to return to Africa one day to help refugees, orphans, and others who are struggling to survive in challenging circumstances.

New citizens wave American flags during a naturalization ceremony in Los Angeles, California, in 2018. At the ceremony, seventy-two hundred immigrants from one hundred nations became US citizens.

"I Am an American Now"

A 2014 study from the American Community Survey focused on five hundred thousand Somali, Burmese, Hmong, and Bosnian refugees in the United States. Analysis of the data showed that most of these refugees achieve a quality of life that corresponds to that of native-born Americans. Many start and run businesses that together earn billions of dollars. After ten years, a majority of refugees have learned English, and many own their homes. After twenty years, three-quarters have become citizens.

Fidel Bahati, born in central Africa, spent almost five years in a Kenyan refugee camp. He knew exactly what he wanted to do when he became a US citizen. Immediately after his naturalization ceremony in late 2017, he enlisted in the US Army Reserves. "I am an American now," he told the *New York Post*. "I will serve my country who has provided me so much opportunity to better myself."

Gaining Employment

Marwan Sweedan also found ways to serve his new country. A doctor in his native Iraq, Sweedan supported US troops during their occupation of his country. Because the US occupation was controversial, he received death threats. After his father was kidnapped and assassinated, he escaped to Jordan with his mother and brothers. In 2008 they came to the United States as refugees. "It was a cultural shock to me coming to the United States," Sweedan later said. "I didn't understand what's going on, and everything was collapsing around me, my world was collapsing."

Sweedan needed to earn a living, but he did not have a license to practice medicine in the United States. Sweedan's first job was selling hot dogs in a mall in San Jose, California. As with other highly educated refugees in low-level, poorly paid jobs, Sweedan was frustrated that he had no outlet for his expertise and knowledge.

Upwardly Global is a nonprofit organization that helps skilled refugees and immigrants find jobs to fit their talents. The organization helped Sweedan get a job in biotechnology. Later, he joined the US Army as a combat medic. Serving in the military also taught him a lot about American politics and culture. When his service ended in 2013, he moved to Idaho. There, he became deeply involved with Global Talent Idaho. This group helps refugees to get jobs that match their education and skills. Working with both organizations, Sweedan launched a task force to connect immigrant doctors with advisers and educational resources. These resources will help immigrant doctors pass the exams and gain the clinical experience they need to get a license to practice medicine in the United States. The task force then helps link them to communities with a shortage of doctors. For Sweedan's work, Obama honored him in 2015 as a White House Champion of Change for World Refugees.

TASHITAA TUFAA

Tashitaa Tufaa was a schoolteacher in Ethiopia. He came to Minneapolis as a refugee in 1992 and took a job as a dishwasher in a large hotel. To support his family, he also worked in a factory. Meanwhile, he was studying for a master's degree in political science and international relations. Still, he was not making enough money to support his family. So he added a night and weekend job driving people with disabilities and senior citizens to work.

Tufaa found the work so satisfying that in 2003, he decided to open his own transportation company. First, he began to work with public school districts to bus children to school. Starting with a single minivan, he began driving homeless children to and from school. By 2017 his company, Metropolitan Transportation Network, boasted three hundred buses and vans. They take fifteen thousand students to school every day all across Minnesota.

"The America You Promised"

Ilhan Omar, the first Somali American lawmaker in the United States, is working toward big social and political changes. When she was eight, her family fled civil war in Somalia. After spending four years in a refugee camp in Kenya, they came to the United States as refugees. At twelve years old, Omar expected all Americans to be happy and successful. She was shocked to see homeless people sleeping on the street in New York City. She saw poor neighborhoods, heaps of trash, and people asking for money. "This isn't the America you promised," she said to her father.

"Well, you just wait," her father said. "We haven't gotten to our America yet."

Omar's family was very interested in government. After they moved to Minnesota, Omar attended political meetings with her grandfather and translated the proceedings for him. "I just fell in love with politics and what it could do," she said. Later, as a student at North Dakota State University, she organized the first Islamic awareness week. Back in Minnesota, she went on to become an aide to

Ilhan Omar came to Minneapolis, Minnesota, as a refugee from Somalia and eventually became a US citizen. In 2016 she was the first Somali American to win a seat in a state legislature. In 2018 she ran for a seat in the US House of Representatives as a Minnesota Democrat. Here she campaigns for that office at the Minneapolis Gay Pride parade in June 2018.

a city council member in Minneapolis. But Omar wanted to do still more. So, in 2016, she ran for the Minnesota House of Representatives.

It was a difficult time for Somali Americans. The week before the election, presidential candidate Trump called Minnesota's large Somali community "a disaster." He wrongly accused some of joining terrorist groups and spreading radical views throughout the country and the world. Most Somalis are hardworking, law-abiding citizens.

Election night left Omar with mixed feelings. She felt excitement and happiness at her own victory and deep disappointment at Trump's election. "My district is one of the most diverse in the nation," Omar told the *New Yorker* magazine the week after the election. "People are afraid. There is an air of sadness and anxiety. As leaders, all we can do is reassure people that we are not going to waver in our fight for them." In 2018 Omar decided to run for a seat in the US House of Representatives as she continues to fight for the America she was promised.

A detained immigrant sits in a holding cell at a US Immigration and Customs Enforcement (ICE) detention facility in Florence, Arizona. Most immigrants at the center are awaiting deportation. Others are held indefinitely while their immigration cases are being reviewed.

CHAPTER SEVEN

ASYLUM SEEKERS IN THE UNITED STATES

Every day asylum seekers without authorization or documentation to enter the United States show up at the US border. Although most are from South and Central America, some migrants from the Middle East and Africa may come to South America first and then head north to seek refuge in the United

States. Customs and Border Protection officers interview, fingerprint, and photograph them. Then they ask the asylum seekers if they fear persecution in their own countries. Economic migrants and others who are not fleeing crime or danger are not allowed into the country. The US Citizenship and Immigration Services will examine the claims of people who do express fears. Officials from this department ask probing questions to assess whether people are telling the truth. If the claims are convincing, asylum seekers have the right to present their case before an immigration judge. The entire process, from border crossing to court hearing, is lengthy.

In April 2018, a caravan (group) of asylum seekers trekking north from Central America, through Mexico, and toward the United States arrived at the border between Mexico and California. Most planned to stay in Mexico, but others wished to apply for asylum in the United States. Criminal gangs had targeted many of these people in their homelands, and they were fleeing for their lives.

Balmore Ramirez Cortez was among the group of asylum seekers. He had lost his brothers to gang violence in El Salvador in 2016 and 2017. Although they did not belong to a gang themselves, a gang killed his brothers because they knew someone in a rival gang. Cortez fled with his two teenage sons because they had received death threats from the gang. He worries about the five-year-old daughter they left behind because she was too young to endure the rigors of the journey. "I'm not going to the United States because I want to," he told the *San Diego Union-Tribune*. "I'm going to the United States to keep my family safe."

Detention Centers

While they wait for their case to be processed, asylum seekers such as Cortez may be held in Immigration and Customs Enforcement-run detention centers. Because of the growing backlog of cases (seven hundred thousand in 2018), asylum seekers may be kept in these centers for more than a year. Conditions in detention centers are often very poor. Homeland Security inspectors went out to five facilities in December 2017. "We identified problems that undermine the protection of detainees' rights, their humane treatment, and the provision of a safe and healthy environment," wrote the inspector general of Homeland Security in his report. These problems included long waits for medical care, unsanitary bathrooms, and abusive attitudes from guards and employees.

Some asylum seekers are released from detention centers through bond hearings held in immigration court. A bond is an agreement through which a person promises to show up for any hearings before a judge. The person pays a certain amount of money for the bond. If the person attends all hearings and follows court orders, that person will receive the money back. In many cases, however, the bond, which may be as much as $15,000, is more than an asylum seeker can pay.

"WE CAN'T GIVE UP"

Mesfin Tesfaldet is a thirty-three-year-old man from Eritrea hoping for asylum in the United States. "We can't give up. We don't have an option," he told the *San Diego Union-Tribune* newspaper. Imprisoned in Eritrea for his political views, Tesfaldet managed to escape to Sudan. He hid for several years, unable to register with the UNHCR because Sudan had an arrangement with Eritrea to return refugees. Finally, he was able to arrange passage to Brazil. But his ultimate goal was the United States. The foot trail from Brazil through the jungle and across rivers to Tijuana, Mexico, on the border of California, was harsh and dangerous. Tesfaldet kept walking. "It was hard," he recalled of the journey. "It's very bad, that jungle. Many people dying, especially in the river." If granted asylum in the United States, Tesfaldet hopes to bring over the five-year-old daughter he left behind in Sudan. He didn't want her facing the dangers of the journey. "I want safe," he said. "I want peaceful."

ASYLUM SEEKERS FLEEING DOMESTIC ABUSE

Domestic abuse and danger from gangs were once a basis for seeking asylum in the United States. In June 2018, the US government changed that policy. US attorney general Jeff Sessions said that any asylum seeker fleeing such situations would have to show that "her home government is unwilling or unable to protect her." Since most asylum seekers do not have an attorney, the challenge of proving this is almost impossible. Sessions also said, "The mere fact that a country may have problems effectively policing certain crimes—such as domestic violence or gang violence—or that certain populations are more likely to be victims of crime cannot itself establish an asylum claim." Thousands of battered and abused women would no longer be able to seek asylum in the United States.

Americans who support the new policy believe it will reduce the caseload in already overcrowded immigration courts. Asylum seekers waiting to cross the border see it as the end of hope. "I'm sickened by a change like this," said Yadira Barrios, who fled from Honduras with her four-year-old son. "My country is a place where gangs extort [squeeze] money from innocents, and if you don't pay you get a shot in the head."

On August 7, 2018, the ACLU sued the US government, alleging that the new restriction placed on asylum seekers was unconstitutional. The lawsuit argues that the policy would cause people "desperately seeking safety [to be] unlawfully deported to places where they fear they will be raped, kidnapped, beaten, and killed." In the midst of the court proceedings, two of the twelve plaintiffs, a mother and daughter, were deported without warning. Federal judge Emmet G. Sullivan of Washington was furious when he learned what had happened. "This is pretty outrageous," he declared. "That someone seeking justice in U.S. court is spirited away while her attorneys are arguing for justice for her?" He ordered the woman and her daughter, already en route to their home country, to be returned immediately. When they landed in Central America, they stayed on their plane and flew directly back to the United States.

JENNINGS V. RODRIGUEZ

Alejandro (Alex) Rodriguez came to the United States as a baby with his parents from Mexico. He became a legal permanent resident and grew up to be a dental assistant and the father of two children. But Rodriguez got into trouble when he was convicted of joyriding (driving dangerously in a car that wasn't his) and possessing illegal drugs. Because he was not a citizen, Rodriguez was scheduled for deportation. He spent three years in a detention facility before the ACLU filed a lawsuit on his behalf. The suit concerned these two important questions: 1) Is the government required to provide bail hearings for aliens (foreigners) held in detention? 2) If not, does this violate the US Constitution?

Eventually, Rodriguez won his immigration case. But the lawsuit filed by the ACLU made its way to the US Supreme Court as *Jennings v. Rodriguez*. (David Jennings was a field office director of the Los Angeles district of Immigration and Customs Enforcement.) In early 2018, the court ruled that the Immigration and Nationality Act of 1965 does not allow regular bail hearings. The court did not rule on the second question, sending it back to a lower court. This court had previously ruled that some immigrants have a right to a bond hearing every six months and that the government must show clear and convincing evidence to keep a person in detention.

Few migrants can afford a lawyer to ensure they receive fair hearings. And unlike other courts, immigration courts do not provide free public defenders (attorneys). Many asylum seekers don't speak English and never learn of their right to a bond hearing. According to a 2014 Stanford University study, two-thirds of the immigrants in detention centers do not have lawyers. Yet Judy London of the Public Counsel Immigrants' Rights Project in Los Angeles says that migrants with lawyers are five times more likely to receive asylum.

Lilian Uriba fled Guatemala to escape violence from drug traffickers who forced her to smuggle illegal substances. Without a lawyer, she faces a hard situation. "If I don't get out [of detention], I won't get the proof I need for asylum. I can't even make a call outside," she told *Rolling Stone* magazine in 2017.

"Competent, Fair Representation"

Elena Albamonte understands both sides of the immigration issue. For three years as an immigration lawyer in Washington, DC, she prosecuted (made the case against) asylum seekers. Her efforts led to hundreds of deportations. In 2011 she moved to an Immigration and Customs Enforcement site in rural Georgia. Once again, her role was to prevent ineligible migrants from gaining asylum. But some cases troubled her. Large numbers of people had no legal help in preparing their cases. Individuals whom she believed *should* get asylum were being denied. Sometimes the reason for this has to do with the location of the immigration court. Georgia as well as North and South Carolina, and parts of Nebraska, Nevada, and Texas have very high rates of denying asylum.

Elena Albamonte moved from the nation's capital to rural Georgia. She is an attorney who works to help asylum seekers. Here, she shakes hands with one of her first clients. He had come to see her from a different state in 2015 to thank her and to introduce his wife and daughter.

ZERO TOLERANCE

In May 2018, US attorney general Jeff Sessions announced a controversial change to US immigration policy. In the past, families caught crossing the border illegally have been released while awaiting a deportation hearing. But Sessions announced a new zero tolerance policy on illegal entry into the United States. "If you cross the border unlawfully . . . then we will prosecute you," Sessions said. "If you smuggle illegal aliens across the border, then we'll prosecute you. If you are smuggling a child, then we will prosecute you, and that child may be separated from you, probably, as required by law."

The US government under Trump believes the rule is necessary to prevent illegal migration. And after the announcement, border patrol agents began taking children from their parents at the border. Children were placed in care facilities with no promise of when they might see their parents again.

Across the nation, Americans were outraged. On June 1, demonstrators gathered in more than two dozen cities to challenge the new policy. "The stories are horrific," said Jessica Morales Rocketto, one of the organizers of the protest in Washington, DC. "It's like, babies being ripped out of their mothers' arms—literally ripped out of their mothers' arms." More than two thousand children were taken from their parents in the first six weeks of the new policy—about forty-six children each day.

On June 20, Trump signed an order reversing the policy of separating families. Instead, the families would be detained together while the adults faced charges for entering the country illegally. But the government didn't keep careful records of the split-up families. The Department of Health and Human Services has case files on 11,800 children. It couldn't readily determine which ones had been separated from their parents under the zero tolerance policy.

Some babies and small children have been taken to distant states while their parents wait for court proceedings. Other children have remained in the United States while their parents were deported. The Trump administration failed to meet a thirty-day deadline for parent-child reunification that a federal judge in San Diego set. As of August 2018, almost five hundred parents could not be located. "And the reality is that for every parent who is not located, there will be a permanently orphaned child," said District Judge Dana Sabraw, "and that is 100 percent the responsibility of the administration."

A child waves at family members from a bus taking migrant children out of a US Customs and Border Protection Detention Center in McAllen, Texas, in June 2018. The US policy of separating families from their children, which went into effect quietly in 2017, soon came to light. Many Americans are enraged by the policy, pointing to the severe trauma the children experience. Others believe it is a fair policy. They say that immigrants with children coming to the United States illegally should be aware of the risks they are taking.

According to statistics from the US Department of Justice, immigration courts in Charlotte, North Carolina, order 84 percent of asylum seekers deported. Yet in San Francisco, only 36 percent are sent back to their homelands. "It is clearly troubling when you have these kinds of gross disparities [big differences]," said Karen Musalo, director of the Center for Gender and Refugee Studies at the University of California's Hastings Law School. "These are life or death matters. . . . Whether you won or whether you lose shouldn't depend on the roll of the dice of which judge gets your case."

Albamonte retired as a prosecutor in 2014 and started a law firm to defend asylum applications. "Not everyone has a right to asylum under the law as it is written," she said. "But everybody does deserve competent, fair representation. That's how the system is supposed to work."

Children of Immigrants

If people feel they have no chance to receive asylum in the United States, they may decide to enter the country illegally. Many people who are poverty-stricken in their own countries hope to find work and a better life for their children in the United States. By entering illegally, these migrants have broken US immigration law. But according to US law, their children had done nothing illegal. Many of these young people grow up in the United States and scarcely remember the country of their birth. The United States is the only home they know. Obama hoped to help these young people with the Development, Relief, and Education for Alien Minors (DREAM) Act. It would have given eligible individuals (known as Dreamers) a chance to apply for US citizenship.

In 2010 the US Congress rejected the DREAM Act. So Obama launched the Deferred Action for Childhood Arrival (DACA) immigration policy in 2012. This allowed people illegally brought to the United States as children to apply for temporary legal status. But it did not offer them a route to US citizenship. If they met certain requirements, Dreamers could stay and work in the United States

Demonstrators in New York City gathered in August 2017 to support DACA.

for two years. After that, they could renew their status. People under DACA could theoretically live in the United States for many years if they kept renewing their DACA application. Obama called the program "a temporary stopgap measure that lets us focus our resources wisely while giving a degree of relief and hope to talented, driven, patriotic young people."

In 2017 Trump canceled DACA, placing eight hundred thousand young people at risk of deportation. The decision sparked nationwide protests and left the Dreamers in legal limbo. "I'm not afraid just for me but for my daughters," explained one woman in North Dakota. She had been covered by DACA, and her US-born children are American citizens. "What is going to happen to them if I am deported?" she asked.

The fate of DACA and the Dreamers already in the United States fell to the courts. Then, on August 3, 2018, a district court in Washington, DC, ruled the DACA program must remain in effect. Judge John D. Bates did not deny that the Department of Homeland Security has the authority to cancel DACA. But, he said, it must present a reasonable explanation for doing so. The arguments already made were not sufficient. The overall future of the program is still undecided.

UNACCOMPANIED CHILDREN

According to UNICEF, more than 300,000 children, most of them unaccompanied, fled their countries between 2015 and 2016. Of these, 170,000 unaccompanied minors sought refuge in Europe, and 100,000 entered the United States at the Mexican border.

Children traveling alone are at high risk. Kidnappers snatch some of them to sell into slavery or sex work. Those who reach their destination often fail to register with the UNHCR and struggle to fend for themselves. Those who do register may spend months or years in a refugee camp without receiving their full legal rights.

In the United States, unaccompanied minors may be held in a childcare center. Others may be placed in the custody of a parent living in the United States, with a relative, or with a sponsor. But many become homeless.

The US government does not provide lawyers to help children make a claim for asylum. Wendy Young is the president of Kids in Need of Defense, a nonprofit organization that helps children get legal representation. According to her, a child with a lawyer has a chance to be granted asylum. This opens up a pathway for citizenship. Without a lawyer, however, Young points out that the approval of a child's asylum application is "virtually impossible."

Girls talk in a dormitory for unaccompanied minors in Shagarab refugee camp in Sudan. Unaccompanied young women are at extremely high risk of kidnapping, sexual exploitation, and rape.

The 2001 earthquake in El Salvador left almost one million people homeless and killed more than seven hundred. Many El Salvadorans have remained in the United States since then, under temporary protected status. Trump revoked that status in 2018, forcing people to decide between remaining illegally in the United States or being deported.

Temporary Protected Status

In January 2018, Homeland Security announced the end of a humanitarian program temporary protected status (TPS) for El Salvador. TPS allows immigrants to remain in the United States when a natural disaster or war has devastated their homeland. El Salvador received TPS when a 7.7 magnitude earthquake, followed by two more major quakes, rocked the country in 2001. To qualify for TPS, individuals must have a clean criminal record and pass a background check. They must pay a fee, and they must be living in the United States when their nation received TPS. Even if they have overstayed their visa or entered the country illegally, they may still apply for TPS.

The US government renewed El Salvador's TPS ten times before it was revoked after Trump became president. The administration argued that TPS was only meant to be temporary. Instead, it had become semipermanent for hundreds of thousands of El Salvadorans. Buildings, roads, and water systems had been repaired in El Salvador.

Trump believed that the reason for TPS no longer existed.

Critics of the cancellation say that many other reasons exist for El Salvador to hold onto TPS. Gang violence and political instability still make the country extremely dangerous. A poor economy and low rate of job creation has caused tens of thousands of people to leave the country. "There's nothing to go back to in El Salvador," Veronica Lagunas told the *New York Times* in January 2018. "The infrastructure may be better now, but the country is in no condition to receive us."

On May 4, 2018, Homeland Security announced the end of TPS for Honduras as well. The country had been granted TPS in 1999, one year after a hurricane had ravaged the nation, killing thousands. Although Honduras has recovered from the hurricane, it has a high rate of violent crime and poverty. The US Department of State cautions Americans not to visit Honduras.

Those who lose their TPS have three options: they can return voluntarily to their country of origin, they can remain in the United States until their date of deportation, or they can continue to live in the United States illegally. But many are willing to risk their hopes on a fourth alternative. It includes a great deal of hardship and uncertainty but has the possibility of a safe haven.

Refuge in Canada

Some people did not wait for Trump to end TPS. From comments he made during his presidential campaign in 2016 and his promise to build a wall on the US-Mexico border, they understood he was not supportive of asylum seekers. His opposition to sanctuary cities (cities that limit their cooperation with immigration policies in order to help migrants) also troubled them. Trump had threatened to withhold federal funds to such cities, but the policy was declared unconstitutional on August 1, 2018.

In contrast, Canada has a reputation for welcoming refugees and for granting more asylum requests than the United States.

NORTH OF THE BORDER

On January 27, 2017, Trump signed the travel ban against seven Muslim nations. The next day, Canadian prime minister Justin Trudeau posted on Twitter a photo of himself greeting a newly arrived Syrian refugee at the airport in Toronto, Ontario. "To those fleeing persecution, terror, & war," wrote Trudeau, "Canadians will welcome you, regardless of your faith. Diversity is our strength."

Between 2011 and January 2018, Canada has accepted fifty-two thousand Syrians for resettlement. During this time, the United States resettled twenty-one thousand. Each country has also accepted several thousand Syrians who entered as asylum seekers without prior vetting.

Canadian prime minister Justin Trudeau greets a Syrian refugee family arriving in Toronto, Canada, in 2015. Three years later, in June 2018, Trudeau criticized the separation of migrant parents and children at the US/Mexican border. "What is happening in the United States is unacceptable. I cannot imagine what these families are going through. Obviously this is not the way we do things in Canada."

Many TPS recipients noticed Prime Minister Justin Trudeau's warm acceptance of Syrian refugees and hoped Canada would take them too. So asylum seekers began heading north toward Canada.

A serious obstacle stood in their way. In 2002 the United States and Canada signed a Safe Third Country Agreement. It requires asylum seekers to apply for refuge in the first country they come to after fleeing their homeland. People who can make it into Canada can still request refuge there. But migrants seeking asylum at an official

Refugees who crossed illegally into Canada from the United States in 2017 line up to enter Olympic Stadium in Montreal, Quebec. The stadium was being used for temporary housing to deal with the large numbers of asylum seekers arriving in Canada from the United States.

border crossing between the United States and Canada will be denied entry because of the agreement. So migrants coming from or through South and Central America must cross into Canada illegally. If they are arrested, they won't be sent back to the United States. The Canadian government gives them a chance to tell their story to an immigration court. In making their case for asylum, they must prove that they have a well-founded fear for their safety if sent back to their home countries.

With tighter immigration policies since the election of Trump, the number of refugees arrested in Canada for illegal border crossings skyrocketed. During Obama's last year in office (2016), twenty-five hundred people were arrested. In 2017 almost twenty thousand people were arrested. The migrants in Canada filled YMCAs and university dorms and spread across the Olympic Stadium in Montreal, Quebec. So many individuals have crossed from New York into Quebec that the route is sometimes called the new Underground Railroad. This refers to the secret network that helped escaping slaves find freedom in Canada in the nineteenth century.

Volunteers in the New York-Quebec border area help migrants bound for Canada—especially during the bitterly cold winter months. Janet McFetridge, who lives just miles from the border, keeps an eye out for those in need of coats, hats, and gloves, which she hands out from her car. "It's . . . offering something that will help them and leaving them with the feeling that there's someone in this country that cares," she said.

Luma Mufleh (*left*) is an immigrant from Jordan. In 2006 she founded Fugees Family in Clarkston, Georgia, to help young survivors of war. She is pictured here with fashion designer Diane von Furstenberg (DVF) at the 2018 DVF Awards in New York City. Each year the award recognizes the work of four women who have shown strength, courage, and leadership skills.

CHAPTER EIGHT

HANDLING THE CRISIS

Clarkston, Georgia, is often hailed as "the most ethnically diverse square mile in America." The town is home to Afghans, Syrians, Iraqis, Vietnamese, Eritreans, Somalis, Ethiopians, Sudanese, Bosnians, Bhutanese, and Burmese residents. "I've been to the future," Mayor Ted Terry said in 2018. "It's multi-ethnic, multi-religious, multi-cultural."

Low-cost housing and good public transportation systems make Clarkston ideal for newly arrived refugees. Few refugees are able to afford a car immediately when they arrive in the United States. But Clarkston's small size means that schools, doctors' offices, the post office, restaurants, and shopping are nearby.

Between 1992 and 2017, Clarkston welcomed more than forty thousand refugees. Most stay a few years before moving on. Mayor Terry describes the community as a "starter city." Once refugees gain financial stability and get used to American customs, many move on to look for better job opportunities or housing.

Hevel Mohamed Kelli came to the United States from Syria in 2001 at the age of seventeen. He started working as a dishwasher. By 2017 he was a respected cardiologist and had moved to a wealthy neighborhood in a nearby town. "Two days after we arrived in Clarkston, we were terrified," Kelli said. "And then all these people arrived at our door with food, wanting to help us learn English. We thought they were the [Central Intelligence Agency] or something, all these white Americans knocking at our door." To the family's relief, the visitors explained they were members of the local Episcopal church. "They didn't look like us," said Kelli. "But they changed our lives."

Italian Towns Revived

Separated by more than 4,500 miles (7,242 km) with a vastly different language and culture, the town of Riace in southern Italy has something in common with Clarkston. Both towns welcome refugees, and the towns have prospered for it. After World War II, people began leaving the agricultural southern part of Italy to seek better jobs in factories in northern Italy. Riace was almost deserted. Then, in 1998, two hundred refugees from the Turkish-Kurdish conflict (in which rebel Kurdish groups demanded freedom from Turkey) landed on a beach near Riace. Exhausted from their hazardous journey, they faced an uncertain future. Mayor Domenico Lucano took immediate steps. "There were people without a house here, and there were houses without people here. It's simple," he said. He offered the migrants shelter, job training, and a warm welcome in Riace. Under Lucano's leadership, the town invited more refugees. Between 1998 and 2016, more than six thousand migrants found hope and safety in Riace.

"THAT UNIVERSAL LANGUAGE"

Luma Mufleh, an immigrant from Jordan, discovered a way to help young people transition to life in the United States and find a sense of belonging in their new country. It happened by accident one afternoon as she was driving home. She took a wrong turn and found herself outside an apartment complex in Clarkston, Georgia, where she saw children playing soccer. Mufleh offered to coach them and help them start a regular team.

The team Mufleh founded in 2004 included players from Syria, Afghanistan, Iraq, Bosnia, Burma, Somalia, Sudan, and other countries. "Soccer is that universal language," Mufleh said. "For kids that were robbed of their childhood [soccer] is one place they get to be kids again. They feel comfortable. They feel confident and happy." By 2018 the original team had grown into the Fugees (short for Refugees) Family. The nonprofit organization includes a school for refugee children in sixth through twelfth grades, a tutoring program, summer camp, and six soccer teams.

Bakeries and workshops in crafts such as glassblowing, ceramics, and embroidery that had been struggling to survive began to prosper again.

Many of the refugees have moved on to bigger cities with broader employment opportunities. But others have found a permanent home in Riace. According to the mayor, people from more than twenty countries made up one-fourth of Riace's 18,500 residents in 2017. By then the welcoming efforts that the mayor had launched had spread beyond Riace's borders. Other declining Italian towns began to grow and thrive with the arrival of refugees and immigrants.

Small towns in other European countries have also benefited from new refugees. But Lucano knows that Riace's success can't necessarily be copied everywhere. He knows that refugee resettlement can be complicated and that many people are suspicious of migrants. Still, he hopes that Riace will provide a model for positive change. He argues against "those Europeans who fear migrants bring disease, take away their jobs and sense of security." Instead, he says that refugees and immigrants "bring us their culture, their world, their colors and their knowledge."

"A Test of Our Humanity"

David Miliband is president and CEO of the International Rescue Committee. This global relief organization provides emergency assistance and long-term help to refugees and displaced persons. Miliband has visited many camps in Africa and the Middle East. His parents were refugees—one of the reasons he took the job with the committee. He says he wouldn't be alive if his parents hadn't escaped Nazi persecution and the genocide (mass extermination) of the Jewish people during World War II. "This is a personal issue for me," Miliband said. "I think in a small way I'm closing the circle and offering some sort of token of thanks to those people who once helped my parents."

At the annual TED (Technology, Entertainment, Design) Conference in 2017, Miliband spoke about the refugee crisis. He said that the crisis is complex and that it can be difficult to solve. But he urged his audience to recognize that solutions to the crisis exist. He spoke about four areas of change to help refugees and lessen the crisis: refugees need jobs, education, money, and, in some cases, resettlement in a Western country. Miliband encouraged his audience to vote for politicians who will create policies to address these areas. He encouraged them to support hiring refugees and to donate money to causes that will provide them with jobs, education, and money. With policies in place to resettle vulnerable refugees in safe countries, they will no longer have to take dangerous journeys across the ocean. And with opportunities to work, become educated, and pay for food and rent, refugees can become more independent, support themselves, and support the local economy.

Miliband believes that Western countries have not only the means but also the duty to welcome refugees. "This is not just a crisis—it's a test," he emphasized at his TED talk. "It's a test of our humanity—of us in the Western world, of who we are and what we stand for. It's a test of our character; not our policies."

HUMANITARIAN CORRIDORS

In February 2016, a Syrian family with a very sick seven-year-old daughter flew to Italy from Lebanon. Spared the hardships and dangers of a perilous ocean crossing, they were the first to benefit from Italy's new Humanitarian Corridors program.

Two months earlier in December 2015, several Catholic and Protestant groups had entered into an agreement with the Italian government to bring a small number of the most vulnerable Syrian refugees to Italy. Several steps are involved in the program. First, Humanitarian Corridors representatives visit refugee camps in selected countries. Working with the UNHCR, they identify refugees most at risk, such as survivors of torture, pregnant women, unaccompanied children, victims of smuggling, and those who are disabled or ill. Screened by the Italian government for security, refugees receive humanitarian visas that grant them entrance into the country and the right to apply for asylum when they arrive.

Second, the refugees are flown directly to Italy. Third, on arrival, they are welcomed into private homes. Volunteers provide Italian lessons, help enroll children in school, and assist adults seeking jobs. "This is a new approach to including refugees in the local community," explained Daniele Albanese of Caritas, an international Catholic relief organization. "We were amazed when a few weeks after launching the project, we had the paradox of more people wanting to help than there were refugees."

Hamdi Ulukaya, founder of Chobani Yogurt, speaks at a conference in San Francisco. He has faced ugly, racist criticism and boycotts of his products because he has stood up for and hired refugees to work in his factories in the United States.

When They Stop Being Refugees

Hamdi Ulukaya came to the United States in the early 1990s from Turkey as a student. After several years, Ulukaya took out a large bank loan to purchase an eighty-five-year-old yogurt factory in Edmeston, New York. He started Chobani Yogurt and created hundreds of jobs. As the need for more employees grew, Ulukaya turned to a resettlement agency in New York that was having difficulty finding jobs for people. But the center's administrators pointed out that few refugees could travel 40 miles (64 km) to his factory each day for work. Many spoke little or no English. So Ulukaya provided transportation and hired translators.

When annual sales of Chobani products reached $1 billion in 2012, Ulukaya opened a second plant in Twin Falls, Idaho. Again, he hired large numbers of refugees, many of them Muslims. People who didn't

REACHING THE YOUNGEST REFUGEES

To help young refugees deal with the trauma of their journeys, the producers of *Sesame Street* and the International Rescue Committee have teamed up. Together they are developing early childhood programs for Syrian refugees. With a $100 million, five-year grant, they will create a Middle Eastern version of the TV show *Sesame Street*. The show will help millions of children master reading and math skills. It will also share social and emotional tools for kids to cope with their situations. Part of the funding will go for home visits. Social workers will provide families with educational games and toys and other materials to help their children do well in school.

Jeffrey Dunn is the president and executive director of the Sesame Workshop (which develops the show). He believes the project may be the most important he has undertaken. "These children are . . . the world's most vulnerable and by improving their lives we create a more stable and secure world for us all," he said.

Afghan puppeteer Mansoora Shirzad records a segment with *Sesame Street*'s new character, a six-year-old Afghan puppet girl called Zari, in April 2016. This will be Zari's first appearance on the local production of the show in Kabul, Afghanistan.

trust Muslims and those who thought the refugees took jobs that should go to US-born workers criticized his actions. Negative commentaries from Breitbart News Network fueled the anger, prompting people to call for a boycott of Chobani Yogurt. Though shaken, Ulukaya stuck to his convictions. "[Refugees] get here legally," he said. 'They've gone through a most dangerous journey. They lost family members. They lost everything they have. And here they are. . . . The number one thing you can do is provide them jobs. The minute they get a job that's the minute they stop being a refugee."

Opposing Viewpoints

Many human rights groups feel that developed Western nations fall far short in their efforts to protect refugees. The split between those who want to welcome refugees and those who fear them persists in the United States and Europe. To many people, the travel ban and the lower annual quota of refugees admitted to the United States indicate a high level of suspicion and intolerance. They feel that such attitudes are unjustified and that America should continue to offer hope and freedom to the oppressed.

Others believe the measures taken by the Trump administration are justified to ensure the safety and economic well-being of all Americans. In Europe some nations have tried to stop migration. Many people fear that large numbers of migrants will negatively change the face of Europe. Other people want to make way for refugees, believing that strength lies in diversity and cultural exchange.

"No Different from Ordinary People"

Wilmot Collins, a refugee of civil war in Liberia, moved to Helena, Montana, in 1994. He had a bachelor's degree in political science and sociology from the University of Liberia in Monrovia and had been active in student government. But he had to become financially

Wilmot Collins, a Liberian refugee, was elected mayor of Helena, Montana, in 2017. He defeated the city's long-term mayor, becoming its first black and first African mayor. He became a US citizen in 2001 and has served in the US military for twenty-two years in the army, army reserve, and navy reserves.

independent as soon as possible to pay his rent. Like all resettled refugees, he had to repay the government the cost of his airplane ticket to the United States. So Collins took a job as a janitor. Twenty-three years later, he was a child protection specialist with Montana's Department of Health and Human Services and a member of the US Naval Reserve. He was also a candidate for mayor. Collins went from neighborhood to neighborhood and knocked on doors to explain his ideas about increasing funding for the police force, firefighting units, and other vital services. Voters responded with enthusiasm. Collins won the election and became the first African and the first black mayor in the state of Montana.

"When I was running, I was not running as a refugee," Collins said. But he does want people to know that criticisms of refugees are unfounded.

"We are not just here to consume resources," he said. "We provide for the economy. I've met so many refugees all around the country—doctors, nurses, social workers, poets, authors, dentists. You name it, they're all over the place. So while I would not say we are all model citizens, we're no different from ordinary people."

A Challenging Road

As long as conflicts continue to erupt and climate change continues to disrupt weather patterns, migrants will be on the move. Turning back boats at sea and closing borders have not solved the crises. When one route to asylum is blocked or made difficult, refugees find other ways to reach their destinations, even if it means more danger and hardship. People are willing to endure a great deal in the hope of a better, safer life.

The solutions that are promising follow the UN Refugee Convention of 1951—upholding refugees' rights to safety, work, health care, and education. But to achieve these goals, experts say that countries with more wealth will have to take some of the pressure off the lesser developed nations that host most of the world's refugees. Humanitarian organizations also urge prosperous nations to provide safe and legal routes to their borders. This prevents refugees from having to place their lives in the hands of corrupt and dangerous smugglers.

Wealthy Western nations can also increase the number of refugees they are willing to resettle. Journalist Patrick Kingsley notes in his book, *The New Odyssey*, that the current crisis is caused not by refugees themselves but by the policies that reject them. Those policies are fueled by strong fears in the United States and Europe that refugees present a danger to national security. Some people feel threatened by people from different cultures and oppose the resettlement of those refugees in their countries. They do not view diversity as a strength but as a weakness.

Compared to the European Union's overall population of about 500 million people, the 850,000 refugees who crossed European

Union borders in 2015 do not represent a huge number. Kingsley believes Europe has room for the refugees, who will create new lives and integrate into new cultures. The same is true of the United States. Many people, including UNHCR chief Filippo Grandi, would like to see the United States reverse its policy of drastically lowering the quota for refugees. He hopes the United States will become a leader in welcoming refugees to its shores.

YOU CAN HELP

There are many things that you can do to help refugees in your community. Here are a few ideas from the UNHCR:

- Make friends with refugee students at your school. Invite them to join activities. Explain what they can expect in class and at school events.

- Work with a teacher to invite adult refugees to visit your class to talk about their lives before coming to the United States. Ask them to describe what their lives are like and what they hope for in the future.

- Volunteer to tutor a refugee student in English or another subject. Your school or local library may have tutoring programs that you can join. If not, look online for other tutoring programs where you live.

- Create a school display that explains the causes of the refugee crisis and the hardships that displaced people endure.

- Write letters to local politicians and to your US senators and representatives. Or send emails to their offices. Urge them to sponsor legislation that supports refugees.

Until developed countries accept more refugees, hundreds of thousands of people will remain in camps or will struggle to eke out a living in crowded cities. "If you look at the statistics, you get depressed," said David Miliband in 2017. "If you look at the people, you have hope. If they don't give up, then we have no right to give up either."

- Hold a fund-raising event at your school and donate the money to a refugee organization your school supports. The money may go toward medicine, clothing, and school supplies for refugee families.

The Reverend Debbie Buchholz (*center*) is hard of hearing. She leads an American Sign Language class for deaf refugees in Kansas City, Kansas. Volunteer tutor John Kingsley (*right*) helps Buchholz with the class, which is part of a program for deaf refugees at her church.

SOURCE NOTES

4   Oscar Lopez, "Pope Francis Calls for World Action on Refugees in Visit to Greece," *Time,* April 16, 2016, http://time.com/4296723/pope-francis -refugees-lesbos-greece/.

5   "Pope Francis' Full Speech in a Moria Refugee Camp (Lesbos)," Rome Reports, April 16, 2016, https://www.romereports.com/en/2016/04/16 /pope-francis-full-speech-in-moria-refugee-camp-lesbos/.

5   Eli Meixler, "'Let's Not Extinguish Hope in Their Hearts. Pope Francis Calls for Empathy toward Migrants and Refugees," *Time,* January 2, 2018, http://time.com/5083672/pope-francis-new-year-message-migrants-refugees/.

5   "UNHCR Viewpoint; 'Refugee' or 'Migrant'—Which Is Right?," UNHCR, July 11, 2016, http://www.unhcr.org/en-us/news/latest/2016/7/55df0e556 /unhcr-viewpoint-refugee-migrant-right.html .

6   Bill Weir, "Can Pope Francis Keep the Door Open for Refugees?," *CNN,* updated March 23, 2018, https://www.cnn.com/2018/03/23/world/pope -francis-syrian-refugees-bill-weir/index.html.

6   Weir.

6   ANSA, "Dreams of a Normal Childhood for Her Son," InfoMigrants, May 7, 2017, http://www.infomigrants.net/en/post/2796/dreams-of-a-normal -childhood-for-her-son.

8   Matthias von Heim, "Climate Change: A Catalyst for Conflict," DW, November 6, 2016, https://www.dw.com/en/climate-change-a-catalyst-for -conflict/a-41245925.

9   Carolyn Kormanan, "Tangier, the Sinking Island in the Chesapeake," *New Yorker,* June 8, 2008, https://www.newyorker.com/news/dispatch /tangier-the-sinking-island-in-the-chesapeake.

9   Damian Carrington, "Climate Change Will Stir 'Unimaginable' Refugee Crisis, Says Military," *Guardian* (US ed.), December 1, 2016, https://www .theguardian.com/environment/2016/dec/01/climate-change-trigger -unimaginable-refugee-crisis-senior-military.

10   Tim McDonald, "The Man Who Would Be the First Climate Change Refugee," *BBC,* November 5, 2015, https://www.bbc.com/news/world -asia-34674374.

10   Jonathan Pearlman, "New Zealand Creates Special Refugee Visa for Pacific Islanders Affected by Climate Change," *Singapore Straits Times,* December 9, 2017, https://www.straitstimes.com/asia/australianz/new-zealand-creates -special-refugee-visa-for-pacific-islanders-affected-by-climate.

11   "Why UNHCR Is Taking Action on Climate Change," UNHCR, accessed August 13, 2018, http://www.unhcr.org/innovation/why-unhcr-is-taking -action-on-climate-change-displacement/.

14 Yusra Mardini and Josie Le Blond, *Butterfly: From Refugee to Olympian—My Story of Rescue, Hope, and Triumph* (New York: St. Martin's, 2018), 201.

14 "Courageous Syrian Swimmer Named UN Refugee Goodwill Ambassador," *U.S. News,* April 27, 2017, https://news.un.org/en/story/2017/04/556162 -courageous-syrian-swimmer-named-un-refugee-agency-goodwill -ambassador.

17 Cara Giaimo, "The Little-Known Passport That Protected 450,000 Refugees," *Atlas Obscura,* February 7, 2017, https://www.atlasobscura.com /articles/nansen-passport-refugees.

19 Robert Slayton, "Children in Europe Are Europe's Problem," *Commentary,* October 1, 2014, https://www.commentarymagazine.com/articles/children -in-europe-are-europes-problem/.

22 Roger Pulvers, "Chiune Sugihara: Man of Conscience," *Japan Times*, July 11, 2015, https://www.japantimes.co.jp/news/2015/07/11/national/history /chiune-sugihara-man-conscience/#.W0_TUmUddE4.

23 "Convention and Protocol Relating to the Status of Refugees," UNHCR, accessed July 18, 2018, http://www.unhcr.org/en-us/3b66c2aa10.

24 "Franklin D. Roosevelt 1941 State of the Union Address 'The Four Freedoms,' (6 January 1941)," Voices of Democracy, accessed July 18, 2018, http://voicesofdemocracy.umd.edu/fdr-the-four-freedoms-speech-text/.

24 Mary Robinson, "Refugees Magazine Issue 111 (Universal Declaration of Human Rights 59th Anniversary)—Welcoming the Downtrodden," UNHCR, March 1, 1998, http://www.unhcr.org/en-us/publications /refugeemag/3b80e2a74/refugees-magazine-issue-111-universal-declaration -human-rights-50th-anniversary.html.

27 Rupert Colville, "Fiftieth Anniversary of the Hungarian Uprising and Refugee Crisis," UNHCR, October 23, 2006, http://www.unhcr.org/en-us /news/latest/2006/10/453c7adb2/fiftieth-anniversary-hungarian-uprising -refugee-crisis.html.

29 "LBJ on Immigration—President Lyndon B. Johnson's Remarks at the Signing of the Immigration Bill, Liberty Island, New York," American Presidency Project, October 3, 1965, http://www.presidency.ucsb.edu /ws/index.php?pid=27292.

29 "LBJ on Immigration."

30 "Resettling Vietnamese Refugees in the United States," *National Geographic,* August 19, 2016, https://www.nationalgeographic.org/media/resettling -vietnamese-refugees-united-states/.

31 Shelby Grad, "As Trump Bans Syrian Refugees, a Look Back at When California Welcomed 50,000 Displaced People," *Los Angeles Times,* January 28, 2017, http://www.latimes.com/local/lanow/la-me-trump -refugees-camp-pendleton-retrospective-20170128-story.html.

33   Edward Walsh, "Effects of 9/11 Reduce Flow of Refugees to the U.S.,"
     Washington Post, August 21, 2002, https://www.washingtonpost.com
     /archive/politics/2002/08/21/effects-of-911-reduce-flow-of-refugees-to
     -us/87c5c2b1-60f2-459a-a96a-50c687dd0a24/?utm_term=.8cdf892c3443.

35   Kriton Capps, "Governors Don't Want Syrian Refugees, Mayors Are
     Asking for Even More," CityLab, November 19, 2015, https://www.citylab
     .com/equity/2015/11/governors-who-dont-want-syrian-refugees-versus
     -mayors-who-are-asking-to-take-more/416718/.

36   Donald J. Trump, Twitter, February 4, 2017, https://twitter.com
     /realdonaldtrump/status/827867311054974976?lang=en.

36   "Timeline of the Muslim Ban," ACLU Washington, accessed July 18, 2018,
     https://www.aclu-wa.org/pages/timeline-muslim-ban.

37   Tim Ryan and Barbara Leonard, "Trump 'Travel Ban' Upheld by
     Supreme Court," Courthouse News Service, June 26, 2018, https://www
     .courthousenews.com/trump-travel-ban-upheld-by-supreme-court/.

38   Lyric Lewin, "In Support of a Travel Ban: People Tell CNN Why They
     Agree with the President's Executive Order," *CNN*, accessed July 18, 2018,
     http://www.cnn.com/interactive/2017/03/politics/travel-ban-supporters
     -cnnphotos/.

38   Lewin.

38   Catie Edmondson, "Sonia Sotomayor Delivers Sharp Dissent in Travel Ban
     Case," *New York Times*, June 28, 2018, https://www.nytimes.com/2018/06
     /26/us/sonia-sotomayor-dissent-travel-ban.html.

38   Edmondson.

39   Kayla Greaves, "Malala Yousafzai 'Heartbroken' over Trump's Immigrant
     and Refugee Ban," Huffington Post, January 30, 2017, https://www
     .huffingtonpost.ca/2017/01/30/malala-yousafzai-trump_n_14500558.html.

41   Rick Gladstone, Megan Specia, and Sydney Ember, "Girl Posting to Twitter
     from Aleppo Gains Sympathy, but Doubts Follow," *New York Times*,
     December 7, 2016, http://www.nytimes.com/world/2016/dec/19/where
     -is-bana-girl-who-tweeted-from-aleppo-is-safely-evacuated.

41   Gladstone, Specia, and Ember.

41   Nadia Khomami, "Where Is Bana? Girl Who Tweeted from Aleppo
     Is Safely Evacuated," *Guardian* (US ed.), December 19, 2016, https://www
     .theguardian.com/world/2016/dec/19/where-is-bana-girl-who-tweeted-from
     -aleppo-is-safely-evacuated.

44   UN Alarmed as US Cuts Aid to Palestinian Refugee Agency," *BBC*,
     January 17, 2018, https://www.bbc.com/news/world-middle-east-42717333.

44   Maayan Lubell, "Israeli Prime Minister Benjamin Netanyahu Calls for
     Dismantling of UN Palestinian Refugee Agency," *Independent* (London),

June 12, 2017, https://www.independent.co.uk/news/world/middle-east
/israel-palestinian-refugee-agency-un-dismantle-benjamin-netanyahu-prime
-minister-a7785146.html.

44 Jaclynn Ashly, "'Without UNRWA We Have Nothing,' Palestinian
    Refugees Speak Out against US Aid Cuts," Mondoweiss, January 25, 2018,
    https://mondoweiss.net/2018/01/without-palestinian-refugees/.

45 Mark Anderson, "Trapped and Bereft in the World's 'Fastest Emptying
    Country,'" *Guardian* (US ed.), September 2016, adapted from an article in
    the *African Report*, https://www.theguardian.com/world/2016/sep/28
    /eritrea-military-service-life-people-left-behind.

45 Sam Jones, Patrick Kingsley, and Mark Anderson, "Escaping Eritrea: 'If I Die
    at Sea, It's Not a Problem—at Least I Won't Be Tortured,'" *Guardian* (US
    ed.), April 21, 2015, https://www.theguardian.com/global-development/2015
    /apr/21/escaping-eritrea-migrant-if-i-die-at-sea-at-least-i-wont-be-tortured.

46 Zachary Laub," Authoritarianism in Eritrea and the Migrant Crisis,"
    Council on Foreign Relations, September 16, 2016, https://www.cfr
    .org/backgrounder/authoritarianism-eritrea-and-migrant-crisis.

47 "Myanmar Rohingya: What You Need to Know about the Crisis," *BBC*,
    April 24, 2018, https://www.bbc.com/news/world-asia-41566561.

47 Gideon Long and Andres Schipani, "Venezuela's Imploding Economy
    Sparks Refugee Crisis," *Financial Times*, April 16, 2018, https://www.ft.com
    /content/a62038a4-3bdc-11e8-b9f9-de94fa33a81e.

48 Nathan Thompson, "The Unwanted: Rohingya Refugees in Bangladesh,"
    CNN, July 16, 2017, https://www.cnn.com/2017/07/16/asia/bangladesh
    -myanmar-rohingya-refugees/index.html.

50 Jean Pierre Balikunkiko, interview with the author, December 13, 2018.

51 Balikunkiko.

53 Davide Lerner, "Turkish Hostility toward Syrian Refugees Rises, Seeps into
    Election," *Haaretz*, May 17, 2018, https://www.haaretz.com/middle
    -east-news/.premium.MAGAZINE-turkish-hostility-toward-syrian-refugees
    -rises-seeps-into-election-1.6096329.

53 Erin Cunningham and Zakaria Zakaria, "Turkey, Once a Haven for Syrian
    Refugees, Grows Weary of Their Presence," *Washington Post*, April 10, 2018,
    https://www.washingtonpost.com/world/turkey-to-syrian-refugees-you
    -dont-have-to-go-home-but-dont-stay-here/2018/04/04/d1b17d8c-222a
    -11e8-946c-9420060cb7bd_story.html?utm_term=.b11ddf3d4a42.

54 ReliefWeb, "'Uganda Has the Most Progressive Refugee Policies in Africa, If
    Not the World,'—UNHCR," Humanitarian Logistics Association, January
    31, 2018, https://www.humanitarianlogistics.org/reliefweb_posts/uganda
    -has-the-most-progressive-refugee-policies-in-africa-if-not-the-world-unhcr/.

54 Jonathan Clayton, "Grandi Praises Uganda's 'Model' Treatment of Refugees, Urges Regional Leaders to Make Peace," UNHCR, January 31, 2018, http://www.unhcr.org/en-us/news/latest/2018/1/5a716d994/grandi-praises -ugandas-model-treatment-refugees-urges-regional-leaders.html.

56 Georgia Graham, "UK Will Not Support Rescue of Mediterranean Migrants," *Telegraph* (London), October 24, 2014, https://www.telegraph .co.uk/news/uknews/immigration/11192027/UK-will-not-support-rescue -of-Mediterranean-migrants.html.

56 "What Happens to Refugees and Stateless Persons Who Have No Passport?," *Uniting Aviation*, January 22, 2018, https://www.unitingaviation .com/strategic-objective/general-interest/refugees-and-stateless-persons -without-passports/.

58 Helena Smith, "Greek Refugee Camps 'beyond Desperate' as Islanders Protest in Athens," *Guardian* (US ed.), December 6, 2017, https://www .theguardian.com/world/2017/dec/06/aid-groups-warn-of-looming -emergency-at-greek-asylum-centres.

58 Nancy Gibbs, "Person of the Year: Angela Merkel: The Choice," *Time*, 2015, accessed October 3, 2018, http://time.com/time-person-of-the-year-2015 -angela-merkel-choice/.

59 "RRDP: Women Fear Violence and Rape in Refugee Camps," *Al Jazeera*, January 24, 2017, https://www.aljazeera.com/news/2017/01/rrdp-women -fear-violence-rape-refugee-camps-170123180556027.html.

61 Madeleine Ngo, "Germany Used to Be a Champion of Open Borders in Europe. Not Anymore," Vox, July 3, 2018, https://www.nationalgeographic .com/photography/proof/2017/10/unaccompanied-minors-refugees-serbia -afghanistan-pakistan-children-migration/.

63 Patrick Kingsley, *New Odyssey: The Story of the Twenty-First Century Refugee Crisis* (New York: Liveright, 206), 179.

66 Agence France-Presse, "Political Dissident Ai Weiwei on Art, Exile, and His Refugee Film Human Flow," *Young Post*, October 20, 2017, https://yp.scmp.com/entertainment/movies/article/107609/political -dissident-ai-weiwei-art-exile-and-his-refugee-film.

66 Ai Weiwei, "The Refugee Crisis Isn't about Refugees. It's about Us," *Guardian* (US ed.), February 2, 2018, https://www.theguardian .com/commentisfree/2018/feb/02/refugee-crisis-human-flow-ai-weiwei -china.

67 Laura Koran, "Trump Administration Dramatically Scales Back Refugee Admissions," *CNN*, September 27, 2017, https://www.cnn.com/2017 /09/27/politics/us-trump-refugee-admissions/index.html.

67 Koran.

67 Oliver Laughland, "Donald Trump Caps Refugee Admissions in 2018 to Historic Low," *Guardian* (US ed.), September 27, 2017, https://www.theguardian.com/us-news/2017/sep/27/donald-trump-caps-refugee-admissions-2018-historic-low.

68 Lauren Gambino, "Trump and Syrian Refugees in the U.S. Separating the Facts from Fiction," *Guardian* (US ed.), September 2, 2016, https://www.theguardian.com/us-news/2016/sep/02/donald-trump-syria-refugees-us-immigration-security-terrorism.

68 "Coming to the U.S. as a Refugee," *CBS News, 60 Minutes,* January 29, 2017, https://www.cbsnews.com/news/60-minutes-the-u-s-screens-syrian-refugees/.

68 "Refugee Admissions," U.S. Department of State, accessed August 5, 2018, https://www.state.gov/j/prm/ra/.

74 Mara Klecker, "At World Refugee Day Celebration in Omaha, 31 Take Oath of U.S. Citizenship," *Omaha World-Herald*, June 25, 2017, https://www.omaha.com/news/metro/at-world-refugee-day-celebration-in-omaha-take-oath-of/article_950b312d-0a33-5edf-904b-cecb6ed104a6.html.

74 Klecker.

75 Balikunkiko, interview, December 11, 2017.

75 Balikunkiko.

76–77 Salena Zito, "This County Voted for Trump and Welcomes Hundreds of Refugees," *New York Post*, January 6, 2018, https://nypost.com/2018/01/06/this-town-voted-for-trump-and-welcomes-hundreds-of-refugees/.

77 Jason Margolis, "Where to Turn When Migrating to America Ruins Your Career," *PRI's The World*, October 27, 2016, https://www.pri.org/stories/2016-10-27/where-turn-when-your-asylum-america-ruins-your-career.

78 Mattie Kahn, "Ilhan Omar Is Still Waiting for the America She Was Promised," *Elle*, March 31, 2017, https://www.elle.com/culture/career-politics/news/a43955/ilhan-omar-interview/.

78 Kahn.

78 Kahn.

79 Ben Jacobs and Alan Yuhas, "Somali Migrants Are 'Disaster' for Minnesota, Says Donald Trump," *Guardian* (US ed.), November 7, 2016, https://www.theguardian.com/us-news/2016/nov/06/donald-trump-minnesota-somali-migrants-isis.

79 Rozina Ali, "A Muslim Woman Also Got Elected Last Week," *New Yorker*, November 17, 2016, https://www.newyorker.com/news/news-desk/a-muslim-woman-also-got-elected-last-week.

81 Gustavo Solis and David Hernandez, "More Immigrants from the Central American Caravan Enter U.S., Few Remain Waiting in Mexico," *San Diego Union-Tribune,* May 3, 2018, http://www.sandiegouniontribune.com/news/immigration/sd-me-carvan-thursday-20180503-story.html.

82 Catherine E. Shoichet, "Surprise Inspections Find 'Significant Issues' in Treatment of ICE Detainees," *CNN*, December 14, 2017, https://www.cnn.com/2017/12/14/politics/immigrant-detainee-treatment-report/index.html.

82 Kate Morrissey, "Asylum Seekers Overwhelming US Processing in San Diego Ports," *San Diego Union-Tribune*, December 26, 2017, http://www.sandiegouniontribune.com/news/immigration/sd-me-asylum-backlog-20171226-story.html.

83 Kevin Johnson and Alan Gomez, "Jeff Sessions: No Asylum for Victims of Domestic Abuse, Gang Violence," *USA Today*, June 11, 2018, https://www.usatoday.com/story/news/politics/2018/06/11/ag-sessions-unveils-strict-asylum-policy-limits-domestic-violence/691978002/.

83 Simon Romero and Miriam Jordan, "On the Border, a Discouraging New Message for Asylum Seekers: Wait," *New York Times*, June 12, 2018, https://www.usatoday.com/story/news/politics/2018/06/11/ag-sessions-unveils-strict-asylum-policy-limits-domestic-violence/691978002/.

83 Nomaan Taxin Merchant and Amy Taxin, "ACLU Lawsuit Accuses US of Wrongfully Denying Asylum," AP News, August 8, 2018, https://apnews.com/543928f0e598448f804ad3d3973592b4.

83 "U.S. Judge Halts Deportation; Threatens Sessions with Contempt," AP News, August 9, 2018, https://www.apnews.com/ee819631ebb545b7814290e2dbb7fd46.

84 Meredith Hoffman, "Trump Era Ushers in New Unofficial Policy on Asylum-Seekers," *Rolling Stone*, April 4, 2017, https://www.rollingstone.com/politics/politics-features/trump-era-ushers-in-new-unofficial-policy-on-asylum-seekers-125308/.

86 Brett Samuels, "Sessions Unveils 'Zero Tolerance' Policy at Southern Border," *The Hill*, May 7, 2018, http://thehill.com/homenews/administration/386634-sessions-illegal-border-crossers-will-be-prosecuted-families-may-be.

86 Joel Rose and Marisa Penaloza, "Protesters across U.S. Decry Policy of Separating Immigrant Families," *NPR*, June 1, 2018, https://www.npr.org/2018/06/01/616257822/immigration-rights-activists-protest-trump-administration-child-separation-polic.

87 Justin Wise, "Judge: Trump Team '100 Percent Responsible' for Reuniting Migrant Families," *The Hill*, August 3, 2018, http://thehill.com/latino/400338-judge-trump-admin-not-aclu-is-100-percent-responsible-for-reuniting-migrant-families .

88 Mica Rosenberg, Reade Levinson, and Ryan McNeill, "They Fled Danger at Home to Make a High-Stakes Bet on U.S. Immigration Courts," Reuters, October 17, 2017, https://www.reuters.com/article/us-immigration-asylum-specialreport/special-report-they-fled-danger-for-a-high-stakes-bet-on-u-s-immigration-courts-idUSKBN1CM1UG.

88   Steve Hendrix, "She Helped Deport Hundreds of Undocumented Immigrants. Now She's Fighting for Them," *Washington Post*, March 28, 2017, http://www.washingtonpost.com/local/she-helped-deport-hundreds -of-undocumented-immigrants-now-shes-fighting-for-them/2017/03 /27/9dc59cc6-04e7-11e7b9fa-ed727b644a0b_story.html?noredirect=on &utm_term=.186a77dd78f6.

89   "Remarks by the President on Immigration," White House, Office of the Press Secretary, June 15, 2012, https://obamawhitehouse.archives.gov/the -press-office/2012/06/15/remarks-president-immigration.

89   Ben Wheeler, "With DACA on Hold, Local DREAMer Lives with Renewed Fears," *Yankton* (*SD*) *Daily Press and Dakotan*, March 13, 2018, https://www .yankton.net/community/article_cc50a51c-2738-11e8-9d56-63f02381b0e3 .html.

90   Rachel Roubein, "Here's How Hard It Is for Unaccompanied Minors to Get Asylum," *Atlantic*, July 15, 2014, https://www.theatlantic.com/politics /archive/2014/07/heres-how-hard-it-is-for-unaccompanied-minors-to-get -asylum/456267/.

92   Miriam Jordan, "Trump Administration Says That Nearly 200,000 Salvadorans Must Leave," *New York Times*, January 8, 2018, http://www .nytimes.com/2018/01/08/us/Salvadorans-tps-end.html.

93   Justin Trudeau, Twitter, January 28, 2017, https://twitter.com/justintrudeau/ status/825438460265762816?lang=en. Accessed August 24, 2018.

93   David Ljunggren and Anna Mehler Paperny, "Canada PM Trudeau pressured to suspend US refugee agreement in face of 'unacceptable' policy, Reuters, June 20, 2018, https://www.reuters.com/article/us-usa-immigration-canada /canada-pm-pressured-to-suspend-u-s-refugee-agreement-in-face-of -unacceptable-policy-idUSKBN1JG24B .

95   Marilla Steuter-Martin, "U.S. Woman Offers Handmade Mittens, Hats to Quebec-Bound Asylum Seekers," *CBC News*, December 10, 2017, https://www.cbc.ca/news/canada/montreal/us-woman-handmade-mittens -asylum-seekers-winter-quebec-border-crossing-1.4441551.

96   Dimitri Lotovski, "Syrian Refugees Settle in Georgia City Known for Diversity," *CBS 46*, January 18, 2016, http://www.cbs46.com/story /30803031/syrian-refugees-settle-in-georgia-city-known-for-diversity.

96   Edward Terry, mayor of Clarkston, GA, interview with the author, May 11, 2018.

97   Terry.

97   Katy Long, "This Small Town in America's Deep South Welcomes 1500 Refugees a Year," *Guardian* (US ed.), May 24, 2017, https://www .theguardian.com/us-news/2017/may/24/clarkston-georgia-refugee -resettlement-program.

97 Long.

97 "Riace: The Italian Village Abandoned by Locals, Adopted by Migrants," *BBC*, September 26, 2016, https://www.bbc.com/news/in-pictures-37289713.

98 Laura Klairmont, "Helping Refugee Kids Find Their Footing in the U.S.," *CNN*, June 10, 2016, https://www.cnn.com/2016/04/14/us/cnnheroes-luma-mufleh-soccer-fugees/index.html.

99 Sylvia Poggioli, "A Small Town in Italy Embraces Migrants and Is Reborn," *NPR*, April 12, 2016, https://www.npr.org/sections/parallels/2016/04/12/473905899/a-small-town-in-italy-embraces-migrants-and-is-reborn.

99 Rob Waugh, "'This Is a Personal Issue for Me,': David Miliband Meets Refugees in South Sudan," *Metro*, June 20, 2017, https://metro.co.uk/2017/06/20/this-is-a-personal-issue-for-me-david-miliband-meets-refugees-in-south-sudan-6722363/.

100 Brian Greene, "'The Duty We Owe to Strangers': David Miliband Speaks at TED2017," *TED Blog*, April 27, 2017, https://blog.ted.com/the-duty-we-owe-to-strangers-david-miliband-speaks-at-ted2017/.

100 "Humanitarian Corridors Are Helping Change How Europeans See Refugees," International Catholic Migration Commission, Brussels, October 23, 2017, https://www.icmc.net/newsroom/news-and-statements/humanitarian-corridors-are-helping-change-how-europeans-see-refugees.

102 Sarah Larimer, "How 'Sesame Street' Will Help Refugee Children and Their Families in the Middle East," *Washington Post*, December 20, 2017, http://www.washingtonpost.com/local/education/how-sesame-street-will-help-syrian-refugee-children-and-their-families/2017/12/20/29075790-e50a-11e7-833-155031558ff4_story.html?utm_term=.a0bd430f390c.

103 Steve Kroft, "Chobani's Billionaire Founder on Creating Jobs in America," *CBS News, 60 Minutes*, June 4, 2017, https://www.cbsnews.com/news/chobani-billionaire-founder-on-creating-jobs-in-america-2/.

104 Corin Cates-Carney, "How a Liberian Refugee Got to Be a Montana Mayor," *NPR*, December 25, 2017, https://www.npr.org/sections/goatsandsoda/2017/12/25/572835450/how-a-liberian-refugee-got-to-be-a-montana-mayor.

107 Waugh, "Personal Issue."

GLOSSARY

anti-Semitism: hostility toward or discrimination against Jews as a religious, racial, or ethnic group

asylum seeker: someone who seeks refuge in a foreign country to escape homeland danger and persecution

climate change: the disruption of atmospheric temperatures and weather patterns due to the large-scale emissions of carbon dioxide and other greenhouse gases into the atmosphere. Greenhouse gases trap the sun's heat and are mostly a result of burning fossil fuels to power cars and factories.

climate migrant: a person displaced from home by severe weather events such as flooding or drought

Customs and Border Protection: a division of the Department of Homeland Security charged with preventing dangerous people, weapons, and materials from entering the United States

Deferred Action for Childhood Arrival (DACA): a US immigration policy put into effect in 2012, giving people brought to the United States illegally as children the chance to apply for temporary legal status. In 2017 Trump announced he planned to phase out the program.

Department of Homeland Security: a US government department founded in 2002 to protect the United States from terrorist activity and to respond to national emergencies

deportation: the removal from a country of a person whose presence is unlawful

detention center: a facility for asylum seekers while they wait for a hearing before an immigration judge

Dublin Regulation: a European Union law stating that the first country in which an asylum seeker arrives is the country responsible for processing the seeker's claim for asylum

economic migrant: a person who enters a country for economic reasons, usually to find better-paying work

Executive Order 13769: a presidential order issued by President Donald Trump in 2017 that restricts the entry into the United States of refugees from seven predominantly Muslim countries. Revised twice, the third and final version of the ban (upheld by the US Supreme Court in 2018) includes Iran, Libya, Somalia, Syria, Yemen, North Korea, and Venezuela. The assumption is that refugees from these nations are more likely to be terrorists than those from other nations.

genocide: a systematic and intentional attempt by a government to murder the entire population of an ethnic, racial, or religious group. In contrast, ethnic cleansing refers to the expulsion of a specific group from a certain region. According to the UN, ethnic cleansing is not considered a crime under international law. Genocide is.

Humanitarian Corridors: a project of the Catholic lay group Sant'Egidio and Protestant churches that allows exceptionally vulnerable refugees to travel safely and legally to Italy. The program was developed in 2015 to protect refugees from human traffickers and dangerous sea journeys.

Immigration and Customs Enforcement: a division of the Department of Homeland Security that enforces immigration law and oversees border controls

internally displaced person: a person who is forced to flee from home but who does not cross an international border

International Rescue Committee: a New York City–based global humanitarian, development, and resettlement agency that helps people affected by war and violence, provides emergency relief to refugees, and helps resettled refugees integrate into their new communities

isolationism: the belief that a country should not be involved with the affairs of other countries, no matter how serious those issues might be

Nansen Initiative: a series of proposals to help people displaced by catastrophic weather events and climate change. The Nansen Initiative has been adopted by 110 governments.

Nansen passport: a post–World War I document that allowed refugees to travel freely between countries. The document was named for its creator, Fridtjof Nansen, high commissioner for refugees for the League of Nations. The closest things to Nansen passports in the twenty-first century are travel documents for stateless people and refugee travel documents.

naturalized citizen: a person who comes to the United States from a foreign country, fulfills all the legal requirements for citizenship, and takes an oath of loyalty to the United States. Naturalized citizens enjoy the same rights and privileges as those born in the United States except the right to be president or vice president.

non-refoulement: a rule that refugees can't be returned to places where they face danger or persecution. The term comes from the French verb *refouler*, which means "to turn back."

refugee: a person who crosses international boundaries to escape homeland violence, civil war, or persecution

refugee camp: a settlement for displaced persons, usually in a host country. The camps are meant to be temporary but often are not. Some are huge, and some are small. Some are overcrowded and dangerous, while others are better maintained and provide more privacy.

Refugee Convention of 1951: a UN treaty that establishes the qualifications for refugee status, sets forth refugee rights, and specifies the responsibilities of countries granting asylum

repatriation: the voluntary or forced return of refugees to a country from which they have fled, often because a host country cannot or does not want to pay the costs of absorbing refugees

sanctuary city: a city with formal and informal policies to help migrants. This may include limiting cooperation with federal immigration enforcement.

smuggler: a person who charges refugees a fee—usually exorbitant—to illegally transport them to another country

temporary protected status: a designation that allows eligible people already in the United States to remain in the country for a limited time due to a natural disaster or political strife in their home country

United Nations High Commissioner for Refugees (UNHCR): a United Nations agency established to promote the protection and well-being of refugees

United States Citizenship and Immigration Services: a division of the Department of Homeland Security that manages naturalization and immigration systems

Universal Declaration of Human Rights: an international document adopted by the United Nations in 1948 that lists basic human rights. It is intended to promote peace.

xenophobia: racial intolerance and fear of foreigners

SELECTED BIBLIOGRAPHY

Bauman, Stephan, Matthew Soerens, and Issam Smeir. *Seeking Refuge: On the Shores of the Global Refugee Crisis.* Chicago: Moody, 2016.

Bennets, Andrew. *The Mess We're In: Managing the Refugee Crisis.* Camberwell, Australia: Trabagem, 2017.

Betts, Alexander, and Paul Collier. *Refuge: Rethinking Refugee Policy in a Changing World.* Oxford: Oxford University Press, 2017.

Griffiths, Rudyard. *The Global Refugee Crisis: How Should We Respond? Arbour and Schama vs. Farage and Steyn; The Munk Debates.* Toronto: House of Anansi, 2016.

Haines, David W. *Safe Haven: A History of Refugees in America.* Sterling, VA: Kumarian, 2010.

Jones, Reece. *Violent Borders: Refugees and the Right to Move.* London: Verso, 2016.

Kingsley, Patrick. *The New Odyssey: The Story of the Twenty-First Century Refugee Crisis.* New York: Liveright, 2017.

Lamey, Andy. *Frontier Justice: The Global Refugee Crisis and What to Do about It.* Toronto: Anchor Canada, 2013.

Miliband, David. *Rescue: Refugees and the Political Crisis of Our Time.* New York: Simon & Schuster/TED Books, 2017.

UNHCR. *The State of the World's Refugees: Fifty Years of Humanitarian Action.* Oxford: Oxford University Press, 2000.

Wennersten, John R., and Denise Robbins. *Rising Tides: Climate Refugees in the Twenty-First Century.* Bloomington: Indiana University Press, 2017.

FURTHER INFORMATION

Books

Abawi, Atia. *A Land of Permanent Goodbyes*. New York: Philomel Books, 2018. A foreign news correspondent, Abawi tells a fictional story of a family's journey from Syria to Turkey and Greece.

Alabed, Bana. *Dear World: A Syrian Girl's Story of War and Plea for Peace*. New York: Simon & Schuster, 2017. Bana and her mother write about life in Syria before and after the civil war.

Behnke, Alison Marie. *Racial Profiling: Everyday Inequality*. Minneapolis: Twenty-First Century Books, 2017. The book includes sections on US counterterrorism policies, the travel ban, Islamophobia, and serious flaws in the FBI watch lists.

Borden, Louise. *The Journey That Saved Curious George: The True Wartime Escape of Margret and H. A. Rey*. Boston: Houghton Mifflin, 2005. The story of the Reys' early lives and their narrow escape from Paris in World War II is illustrated with drawings and photos.

Gratz, Alan. *Refugee*. New York: Scholastic, 2017. This is a fictional story of the coming together of three young refugees—a Jewish boy in the 1930s, a Cuban girl in 1994, and a Syrian boy in 2015.

Hirsch, Rebecca E. *Climate Migrants: On the Move in a Warming World*. Minneapolis, Twenty-First Century Books, 2017. The book covers climate change as a force driving migration and includes information about the efforts of Ioane Teiliota to become the first climate change refugee.

Lee, Sungju. *Every Falling Star: The True Story of How I Survived and Escaped North Korea*. New York: Amulet Books, 2016. Lee recounts how he survived on his own after his parents were forced from their home in North Korea.

McPherson, Stephanie Sammartino. *Arctic Thaw: Climate Change and the Global Race for Energy Resources*. Minneapolis: Twenty-First Century Books, 2015. The book explores the impact of climate change on the Arctic and the consequences for the entire planet.

Miller, Harry. *Refugees*. Philadelphia: Mason Crest, 2017. The book provides a succinct explanation of the refugee crisis.

Park, Linda Sue. *A Long Walk to Water*. Boston: HMH Books for Young Readers, 2011. This award-winning book weaves the stories of Salva, a boy who lives through the 1985 civil war in the Sudan and hardships in refugee camps, and Nya, a girl living in the Sudan in 2008. The book is based on a true story.

Senzai, N. H. *Escape from Aleppo*. New York, London: Simon & Schuster Books for Young Readers, 2018. In this fictional story, Nadia's twelfth birthday coincides with the beginning of the Arab Spring. As civil war erupts and worsens in Syria, Nadia's family must escape as refugees.

St. John, Warren. *Outcasts United: The Story of a Refugee Soccer That Changed a Town.* Young Readers Edition. New York: Spiegel & Grau, 2009. This book tells the story of an immigrant, Luma Mufleh, and how she changed the lives of young refugees near Clarkston, Georgia, by starting an all-refugee soccer team.

Uwiringiyimanna, Sandra, and Abigail Pesta. *How Dare the Sun Rise: Memoirs of a War Child.* New York: Katherine Tegen Books, 2017. This powerful memoir tells the story of a girl's flight from war and persecution in the Democratic Republic of the Congo to resettlement in the United States.

Yousafzai, Malala. *I Am Malala: How One Girl Stood Up for Education and Changed the World.* Young Readers Edition. New York: Little, Brown, 2014. Malala talks about her life in Pakistan, her advocacy for girls' education, and the attack on her life.

Films

After Spring. Directed by Steph Ching and Ellen Martinez. Brooklyn: After Spring, 2016, 1:42. This documentary film focuses on the Syrian refugee crisis and the Zaatari Refugee Camp.

Fire at Sea. Directed by Gianfranco Rosi. Rome: Stemal Entertainment, 21 Uno Film, Istituto Luce Cinecitta, RAI Cinema; Paris: Les Films d'Ici, ARTE France Cinema, 2016. 1:54. Filmed on the Italian island of Lampedusa, this movie deals with refugees' dangerous journeys across the Mediterranean Sea.

The Good Postman. Directed by Toniislav Hristov. Helsinki: Making Movies Oy; Belgrade: Soul Food, 2016. 1:22. A postal worker and candidate for mayor in a small Bulgarian village proposes allowing Syrian refugees to move into the vacant houses to help revitalize the town.

Human Flow. Directed by Ai Weiwei. Los Angeles: Amazon Studios, Participant Media, 2017. 2:20. This film presents powerful refugee stories from across the globe.

The Land Between. Directed by David Fedele. 2013. 1:18. This drama-documentary explores the lives of African migrants living in Morocco.

Pushing the Elephant. Directed by Elizabeth Mandel and Beth Davenport. New York City: Arts Engine, Big Mouth Productions, 2010. 1:31. This documentary tell the compelling story of human rights activist Rose Mapendo, a refugee from Democratic Republic of the Congo who was reunited with her daughter after ten years.

Websites

Global Refugee Crisis
http://www.care.org/emergencies/global-refugee-crisis
This website of the nonprofit agency CARE (Cooperative for Assistance and Relief Everywhere) includes links about the refugee crisis in locations such as Burma (Myanmar), Syria, and the Dadaab refugee camp in Kenya.

Homeland Security
https://www.dhs.gov/about-dhs
The website includes information on securing the borders, DACA, and other issues.

Malala Fund
https://www.malala.org/
This website has links to Malala's story and to the work the fund supports to further education for girls in developing countries such as Pakistan, Lebanon, and Nigeria.

Refugee Rights
https://www.hrw.org/topic/refugee-rights
This website presents information on Human Rights Watch and includes reports and news items on the violation of refugee rights.

Refugee Voices
https://www.refugee-action.org.uk/refugee-voices/
The website presents material about the organization Refugee Action and includes many links to stories of individual refugees.

Rescue.org
https://www.rescue.org
This website explains the work of the International Rescue Committee and includes news and feature stories about the global refugee crisis.

7 Free Short Films about Refugees Recommended by Human Rights Educators
https://www.amnesty.org/en/latest/education/2016/03/seven-free-short-films-about-refugees-recommended-by-human-rights-educators/
The videos include stories of refugees from Syria, Vietnam, and Somalia as well as a segment that imagines Europeans fleeing persecution and seeking refuge in the Middle East and Africa.

UNHCR, the UN Refugee Agency
http://www.unhcr.org/en-us/
The website lists links to current news stories about the global refugee crisis.

US Resettlement Facts
http://www.unhcr.org/en-us/us-refugee-resettlement-facts.html
This UNHCR website presents information about the US resettlement program and includes links to refugee stories.

The World's Five Biggest Refugee Crises
https://www.refugee-action.org.uk/refugee-voices/
This website of Mercy Corps includes information about the crises in Syria, South Sudan, Afghanistan, Lake Chad, and Somalia.

INDEX

PHOTO ACKNOWLEDGMENTS

Image credits: FILIPPO MONTEFORTE/AFP/Getty Images, p. 4; LightRocket/Getty Images, p. 6; Jonas Gratzer/LightRocket/Getty Images, p. 10; Laura Westlund/Independent Picture Service, pp. 12, 64; NurPhoto/Getty Images, p. 13; Independent Picture Service, p. 15; Popperfoto/Getty Images, p. 16; Grethe Ulgjell/Alamy Stock Photo, p. 17; Hulton-Deutsch Collection/CORBIS/Getty Images, p. 18; Popperfoto/Getty Images, p. 20; AF Fotografie/Alamy Stock Photo, p. 24; National Archives, p. 24; Keystone Pictures USA/Alamy Stock Photo, p. 26; Stan Wayman/The LIFE Picture Collection/Getty Images, p. 29; Fred Ihrt/LightRocket/Getty Images, p. 30; George Rose/Getty Images, p. 31; Hristo Rusev/NurPhoto/Getty Images, p. 34; Ronen Tivony/NurPhoto/Getty Images, p. 37; RJ Sangosti/The Denver Post/Getty Images, p. 39; Emre Senoglu/Anadolu Agency/Getty Images, p. 40; Volkan Furuncu/Anadolu Agency/Getty Images, p. 41; FETHI BELAID/AFP/Getty Images, p. 42; Sam Tarling/Corbis/Getty Images, p. 44; Sally Hayden/SOPA Images/LightRocket/Getty Images, p. 45; zakir hossain chowdhury/Barcroft Media/Getty Images, p. 48; AP Photo, p. 50; Stephen J. Boitano/LightRocket/Getty Images, p. 52; Samuel Nacar/SOPA Images/LightRocket/Getty Images, p. 55; ALFONSO DI VINCENZO/AFP/Getty Images, p. 57; Louise Gubb/Corbis/Getty Images, p. 59; Lukas Barth/Anadolu Agency/Getty Images, p. 60; Sean Gallup/Getty Images, p. 61; Owen Humphreys/PA Images/Getty Images, p. 63; Toby Zerna/Newspix/Getty Images, p. 65; Sean Gallup/Getty Images, p. 73; AP Photo/Don Ryan, p. 74; © Richard A. McPherson, p. 75; Mario Tama/Getty Images, p. 76; Craig Lassig/ZUMA Wire/Alamy Live News/Alamy Stock Photo, p. 79; John Moore/Getty Images, p. 80; Michael A. Schwarz/For the Washington Post/Getty Images, p. 85; Spencer Platt/Getty Images, p. 86; Jeenah Moon/Bloomberg/Getty Images, p. 89; Sally Hayden/SOPA Images/LightRocket/Getty Images, p. 90; YURI CORTEZ/AFP/Getty Images, p. 91; AP Photo/Nathan Denette/The Canadian Press, p. 93; AP Photo/The Canadian Press, p. 94; Steven Ferdman/Patrick McMullan/Getty Images, p. 96; Mike Windle/Getty Images for Vanity Fair, p. 101; AP Photo/Rahmat Gul, p. 102; William Campbell/Corbis/Getty Images, p. 104; Allison Long/Kansas City Star/TNS/Getty Images, p. 107.

Cover: Kevin Frayer/Getty Images AsiaPac.

ABOUT THE AUTHOR

A former teacher and journalist, Stephanie Sammartino McPherson has written more than thirty books. Her award-winning titles for YA readers include *Iceberg Right Ahead: The Tragedy of the Titanic, Arctic Thaw: Climate Change and the Global Race for Energy Resources, Doping in Sports: Winning at Any Cost?,* and *Artificial Intelligence: Building Smarter Machines.*